TEACH YOURSELF BOOKS

Golf

Golf

Bernard Gallacher & Mark Wilson

TEACH YOURSELF BOOKS

All the photographs in the colour section were supplied by ALLSPORTS

For UK orders: please contact Bookpoint Ltd, 39 Milton Park, Abingdon, Oxon OX14 4TD. Telephone: (44) 01235 400414, Fax: (44) 01235 400454. Lines are open from 9.00 – 6.00, Monday to Saturday, with a 24 hour message answering service. Email address: orders@bookpoint.co.uk

For U.S.A. & Canada orders: please contact NTC/Contemporary Publishing, 4255 West Touhy Avenue, Lincolnwood, Illinois 60646 – 1975 U.S.A. Telephone: (847) 679 5500, Fax: (847) 679 2494.

Long-renowned as the authoritative source for self-guided learning – with more than 30 million copies sold worldwide – the *Teach Yourself* series includes over 200 titles in the fields of languages, crafts, hobbies, sports, and other leisure activities.

British Library Cataloguing in Publication Data
A catalogue record for this title is available from The British Library

Library of Congress Catalog Card Number: 92-82519

First published 1985; second edition first published in UK 1997 by Hodder Headline Plc, 338 Euston Road, London NW1 3BH.

First published in US 1997 by NTC/Contemporary Publishing,
4255 West Touhy Avenue, Lincolnwood (Chicago), Illinois 60646-1975 U.S.A.

The 'Teach Yourself' name and logo are registered trade marks of Hodder & Stoughton Ltd.

Typeset by Transet Limited, Coventry, England.
Printed in Great Britain for Hodder & Stoughton Educational,
a division of Hodder Headline Plc, 338 Euston Road, London NW1 3BH
by Cox & Wyman Limited, Reading, Berkshire.

Impression number	14	13	12	11	10	9	8	7	6	5	4		
Year			2004	2003	2002	2001	2000	1999	1998				

CONTENTS

INTRODUCTION

The appeal of golf has spread throughout the world to give enjoyment to many millions, and their numbers continue to grow each day. For all players the game provides a continual challenge to learn from one's mistakes. There are the comparative few who have developed an enviable talent to play the game exceedingly well. But the 'average golfer' can derive as much pleasure from his modest successes as the expert does from his mightier achievements, and it is this fact that begins to explain the true appeal of golf.

In the first instance, golf answers the need in everyone's nature to be competitive. Golf is all about competing and the game's unique handicapping system allows any novice playing to the best of his ability, a chance to give a champion a good match, even to beat him on occasions. It is this facet for bringing the beginner and the accomplished player together on equal terms that places golf apart from other sports. Through the ages a great many people have attempted to define the qualities of golf. Something like a century ago David R. Forgan, who came from the Scottish family of club makers, gave his interpretation and no better definition has been seen since. He wrote:

'Golf is a science, the study of a lifetime, in which you may exhaust yourself but never your subject.

'It is a contest, a duel or a mêlée, calling for courage, skill, strategy and self-control.

'It is a test of temper, a trial of honour, a revealer of character.

'It affords a chance to play the man, and act the gentleman.

'It means going into God's out of doors, getting close to nature, a fresh air exercise, a sweeping away of the mental cobwebs, genuine recreation of the tired tissues.

'It is a cure for care – an antidote to worry.

'It includes companionship with friends, social intercourse, opportunity for courtesy, kindliness and generosity to an opponent.

'It promotes not only physical health but moral force.'

— Every golfer is his own referee —

Quite simply, golf holds every type of challenge. And, of course, it is the game of a lifetime. It can be taken up at the age of six and enjoyed to eighty and beyond. It is a game that prospers all the more for the importance it places upon pride. The newest recruit to the game will share the pride and sense of satisfaction felt by an Open champion, when he hits a good shot. A beginner may well tee up the ball and mis-hit it fifty times but eventually he hits a good shot and at that moment his sights are set for the future. He knows that he has it in him to do it, and the challenge is there to be met. Certainly, it is a great test of character and of honesty. Every golfer is his own referee and on this understanding the game has remained one of the most honourable of all sports.

The learning of golf lasts a lifetime, and always remains an unfinished exercise; the greatest golfers freely admit they are constantly learning something new each day, and Open champions are the first to declare that perfection in golf is an impossible dream. Improvement is a realistic challenge at all levels.

To succeed in this task means, in the beginning, a thorough learning of the fundamentals of the game and this, we must emphasise, is best done with a professional golfer. Lessons from a good teacher are invaluable to the novice, but once on the right road, you can start to teach yourself, and this book will help you progress swiftly in the right direction. Expert guidance as you first learn is essential, and without it you will almost certainly develop bad habits which will plague your golf and deny you full enjoyment of the game.

Tuition in itself is not enough, however. You must also do a great deal for yourself. Once you understand the fundamentals, then you can build on them – and that means many hours of working on the game alone. It is at this stage that you will find this book most helpful. Take it to the practice ground for immediate reference, and make efficient use of the material by concentrating on one section at a time.

Experiment to learn

The most effective way of learning is to experiment. The object is simple enough: to learn how to hit the ball consistently well enough to enjoy the game. Practice is an art in itself; it has to be carried out intelligently and with a prepared purpose. There is no sense hitting a hundred golf balls aimlessly. Little more is achieved that way than the exercising of muscles. When these tire, mistakes, bad habits and costly faults are built into the golf swing for future punishment. The golfer who practises intelligently will find his dedication neither dull or monotonous, but rewarding.

1
CHOOSING YOUR EQUIPMENT

The equipment

When taking up the challenge of golf the choosing of the right equipment is as essential as it is simple. Take advice from a professional's shop; mistakes are costly, and as bad tools will always create a bad workman, so will bad clubs produce a bad golfer.

The clubs

In the beginning there is absolutely no need to buy a full set of 14 clubs involving an outlay of hundreds of pounds. Seven clubs can suffice for a while, a 3 wood, then say, numbers 3, 5, 7, 9 irons, a sand wedge and a putter. (See Figure 1.)

It is important to match the lies (determined by the angle between the clubhead and the shaft – see Figure 2, page 8) and the lofts (the angle of the clubface – see Figure 3, page 9). Whatever number of clubs you choose to play, do form a truly balanced set and not a collection of oddments. The same applies to a constant swing weight which gives each club an identical 'feel' in the hands. Considerable care has also to be taken in selecting the right flex and length of club shaft. It is like putting an engine together – if one component is faulty then the rest have no chance of performing to their full potential.

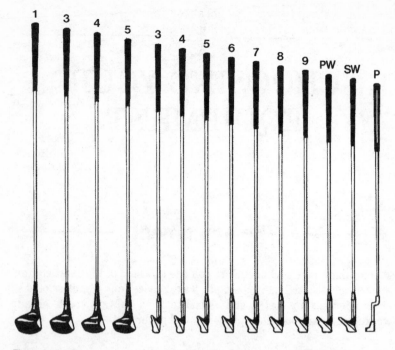

Fig. 1 A popular composition of a full set of 14 clubs, the maximum number allowed by the rules.
Left to right. Nos 1, 3, 4, 5 woods, Nos 3–9 irons, pitching wedge, sand wedge and putter. As the loft increases, the length of the shaft decreases.

Happily, the task of buying the right equipment is considerably easier now than it was some years ago when hickory shafts made the collection of a matched set a lifetime pursuit. Today the manufacturers bear the burden and unless you are of extremely abnormal physique there is a factory-made product instantly suited to your needs. Even so, there is still the first hurdle to be surmounted: deciding exactly what it is that best suits you as an aspiring golfer.

There are different ways to tackle this problem. The first is, naturally, to consult the professional at your golf club or driving range. He can give you the same attention and detailed advice as a tailor fitting you for an expensive suit. Some manufacturers are happy to lend, through club professionals, a sample of their products for use on the practice ground. In the same way that it would be most unwise to buy a new car without a test run, so the golfer seeking a set of clubs should insist on some form of trial to help him make his final choice.

If you have friends who are golfers already don't hesitate to ask them for a loan of their clubs before making a final choice. Again, if you are thinking of buying a second-hand set of clubs to get started – and there is absolutely nothing wrong in this – and your professional has something on offer, arrange to use them on a trial basis. Whatever you do, don't buy a set of expensive clubs simply because you like the look of them.

In the selection process there are general guidelines to help. The shaft is the most important part of the club and there are a number of different designs with varying weights and flexes from which to choose. If you get it right, playing golf becomes much simpler; get it wrong and your struggles with unsuitable equipment will take the enjoyment out of the game quite quickly. As a generalisation, the stiffer the shaft the greater chance you have of hitting the ball straight. Increased flex to make the shaft 'whippy' is an aid to hitting the ball a greater distance. But it is not a simple matter. Your physique and temperament as a golfer play a large part in deciding which of the two shafts is best for you. If, for example, you have comparatively weak hands, then the kind of stiff shafts used by tournament professionals will cause you nothing but trouble. They will have a stiff 'poker' feeling and it will be impossible for you to achieve the all-essential clubhead speed through the ball at impact. For an extreme example, try swinging a broom like a golf club, and then a thin cane. Obviously, the cane will 'swish' through the air at a much faster rate. Conversely, if you have the natural asset of strong hands then a club that has a shaft with too much flex is the wrong choice. The tendency is to 'whip' the clubface out of line, and then the ball can go in any direction.

If your natural tendency is to rush through life, to run rather than walk, you are likely to have a fast swing, in which case you are more likely to find success with a heavier, stiffer club shaft. If you have a slow, smooth swing then the extra whip of a more flexible shaft should be considered. Discovering which of these many shafts is best suited to your needs is most effectively done by taking an hour on the practice ground with examples of each type.

Beware the temptation to tinker with the idea of having club shafts shorter or longer than standard. It may seem sound in theory, and it is a thought that comes to all beginners, but you really have to be of

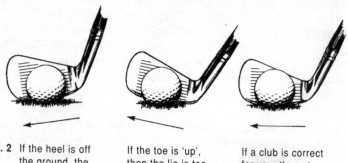

Fig. 2 If the heel is off
the ground, the
lie is too flat for
you.

If the toe is 'up',
then the lie is too
upright for you.

If a club is correct
for you, then at
address the
clubhead lies flush
on the ground.

unusual build to require the lengthening or shortening of shafts. The different needs of short and tall players are met through adjusting the lie of a club and that poses no problem to the professional who has a special gadget in his shop for that very purpose.

Attention to detail is never more important than when determining the thickness of the rubber or leather grips on your set of clubs. A youngster struggling with grips intended for an adult with large hands can develop bad habits that plague him for years; indeed, posture has a knock-on effect that can damage your whole game. Think carefully about every item of equipment. Do not be tempted into starting with a straight faced (strong) driver in an attempt to power the ball prodigious distances from the tee. That comes later. The No. 3 wood with its customary 14 degrees of loft will best serve the learner. He needs a club that is going to help him sweep the ball into the air. Which particular irons to choose for a 'short' set is another matter of personal preference. Most beginners settle for the 3, 5, 7, 9, sand wedge and putter to go with their No. 3 wood. But there is nothing to say you shouldn't select the 4, 6, 8 and wedge as alternative irons. Figure 3 shows the average degrees of loft for normal woods and irons. What should be accepted is that seven clubs are enough for a start. They can always be 'matched up' later to make a full set. In accepting this, there is absolutely no fear of feeling embarrassment when playing alongside others who may be carrying the full complement of 14 clubs allowed by the rules. The power of positive thinking plays a great part in golf and in this respect it is as well to remember

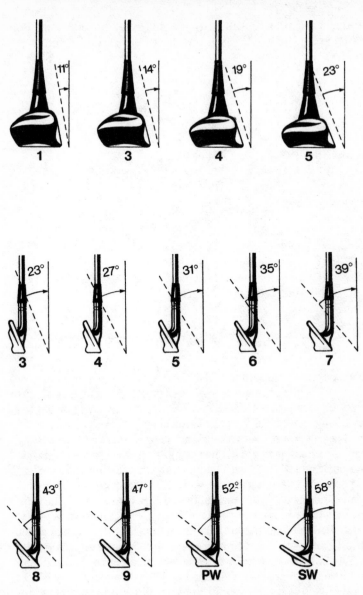

Fig. 3 Average degrees of loft for the most popular woods and irons.

that Harry Vardon, one of the greatest golfers in history, won the Open Championship six times – and he rarely carried more than seven clubs.

	Club		
	No. 1	11 degrees	Driver
	No. 3	14 degrees	3 Wood
Woods	No. 4	19 degrees	4 Wood
	No. 5	23 degrees	5 Wood
Long irons	No. 2	20 degrees	
	No. 3	23 degrees	
	No. 4	27 degrees	
Medium irons	No. 5	31 degrees	
	No. 6	35 degrees	
	No. 7	39 degrees	
Short irons	No. 8	43 degrees	
	No. 9	47 degrees	
Pitching wedge		52 degrees	
Sand wedge		58 degrees	

The balls

After making the right choice of clubs there is the importance of deciding which of the many brands and designs of golf ball on the market is right for you. The answer, again, is very much a matter of personal preference, and what you can afford. There are four main alternatives beginning with the high compression ball favoured by tournament professionals. This has a thin Balata covering and inside there is another ball filled with liquid wrapped in a seemingly endless band of rubber. The characteristics of this ball promote maximum distance and spin as an aid to controlling its flight. At impact, the comparatively soft Balata covering stays fractionally longer on the clubface. But for the same reason it is much, much easier to damage or 'cut' the ball and this can prove expensive for the beginner. At the other end of the range on offer is the solid ball, a composition of tough synthetic rubber materials resistant to damage. Inevitably, it is also resistant to spin and therefore all the more difficult to control on hitting the ground. There is also what is known as the two-piece ball, a synthetic centre covered by Surlyn, and a fourth type which has a wound centre covered by Surlyn, particularly recommended for novices as offering the best of all worlds.

Shoes and clothing

There are very many different kinds of golf shoe but the basic choice is between spikes and rubber soles. On the whole, the best golfers prefer traditional spikes. The golf swing has to be built on a firm base, with no slipping or sliding, and spikes most certainly answer this need. This is not to say, however, that the rubber-soled lighter golf shoe does not have its usefulness on a dry summer's day.

Clothing, naturally, is a matter of personal preference up to a point. You will probably find it a worthwhile investment to purchase a golfing sweater which provides a degree of waterproof protection. As in any sport, your clothes should fit comfortably so as not to restrict your movements, but it should be recognised by every beginner that golfers pride themselves as being among the smartest of all sportsmen. This is not a matter of vanity – as you will find, the golfer who feels smart and tidy in his appearance will also tend to apply the same high standards to his game on the course.

2
GETTING A GRIP ON THE GAME

——— The fundamentals of golf ———

By the fundamentals of golf we mean how to grip the club, stand to the ball properly, and how to groove the backswing and downswing into one finely balanced and co-ordinated movement of controlled power. The learning process will be greatly accelerated by watching others who are proficient at the game, especially the best tournament professionals.

It would be an act of kindness to deny any beginner the right to leave the practice ground for the golf course itself until he had made a habit of gripping the club correctly. There is no such thing as any one 'secret' to success in golf, but there is certainly a single factor which can guarantee perpetual trouble, and that is a bad grip. Among average golfers, only one in six, it is said, has anything like a proper grip, and this goes a considerable way to explaining the problems of the great majority. In fact, mastering a good grip is, basically, very simple, and if you take the trouble to learn this early on, you will have every chance to make the most of your ability, and enjoy the game as it should be enjoyed. Neglecting to acquire a good grip will condemn you to unceasing frustration. The right grip is the key to all progress; fail to recognise this and you will spend your whole golfing life trying to compensate for it. In turn, compensations lead to the development of the wrong arm muscles, and after a while, it is difficult, perhaps even possible, to make amends. So, getting it right at the start is imperative.

The observance of several golden rules is required to acquire a grip that will not only allow but actively encourage a good swing and successful golf. Firstly, it has to be understood that although the club is 'held in the hands', it is actually gripped by the fingers of the right hand and the palm of the left. Often, too much emphasis is placed upon power in golf, and too little is thought about 'feel' and 'touch' which are equally important. The big muscles of the arms, shoulders and legs can generate most of the energy needed to power the shot, while the sensitive fingers bring the critical factor of 'feel' into play.

The next golden rule to understand, learn and practise until its observance becomes second nature, is that the two hands must work as a single unit. They should be equal partners, sharing their workload; if one dominates then the whole balance of the swing is destroyed, and you have a guaranteed recipe for turning a game of golf into a perpetual search for the ball.

The techniques of the grip

As shown in Figure 4, there are three basic methods from which the beginner can choose; the *Vardon* grip, the *interlocking* and the *doublehanded* (often referred to as the baseball grip).

The Vardon grip

This is the most popular by far and it is to be recommended to all with normal-sized hands. Place the left hand on the shaft of the club so that it lies on a diagonal line running from the middle joint of the first finger to about an inch above the little finger, so nestling under the muscular pad of the palm (Figure 5). Close the fingers as if shaking hands, ensure that the **V** formed by the thumb and forefinger is pointing midway between the chin and right shoulder, and that part of the grip has been perfected (Figure 6).

The next move is to hold the club in the fingers of the right hand (Figures 7 and 8) which is then wrapped over the left so that the palm covers the left thumb. The little finger slides into the groove between the left forefinger and the middle finger, and the other three fingers

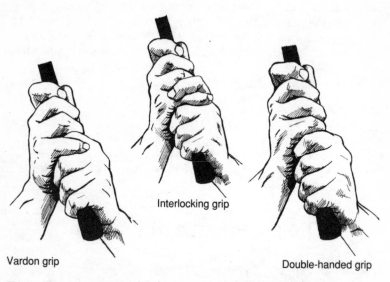

Interlocking grip

Vardon grip

Double-handed grip

Fig. 4 Three methods with the same objective; to make both hands work as one unit.

of the right hand grip the club. Again, the **V** of the right hand should be pointing slightly right of the chin. The right forefinger should feel as though the top joint is gently squeezing the trigger.

When the grip is right, the back of the left hand and the palm of the right will both, along with the face of the club, be square to the target. This is absolutely essential. Another basic requirement is that preferably two, and certainly no more than three, knuckles should be showing on the left hand. This promotes a 'neutral' grip and opens the way to consistent, good golf (Figures 9 and 10). The pressure points in the hand should be felt between the left thumb and the palm of the right hand.

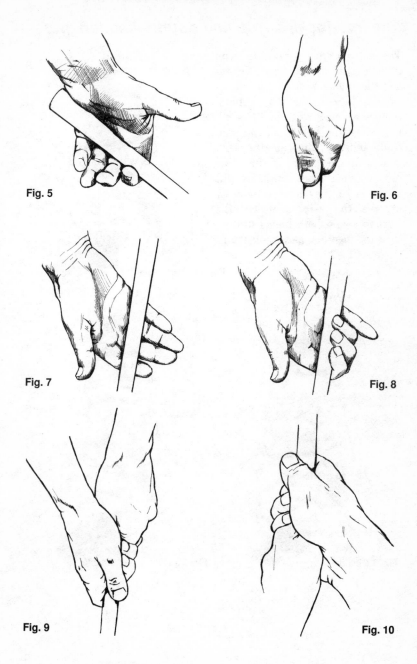

Fig. 5

Fig. 6

Fig. 7

Fig. 8

Fig. 9

Fig. 10

The interlocking grip and double-handed grip

The alternative *interlocking* grip, good for those with short fingers and the *double-handed* grip, which can be helpful for lady golfers, juniors or men with small, weak hands, are no bar to playing golf well. Indeed, some of the best golfers in the history of the game have employed these methods. But in doing so they have religiously observed the basic essentials of the Vardon grip – both hands uniting to work together as a single unit (Figures 11–13).

Fig. 11 Vardon grip.

Fig. 12 Interlocking grip.

Fig. 13 Double-handed grip.

Even the best and most correct of grips can be ruined if the club is held too tightly or too loosely. Tightness promotes tension, and if the club is held so loosely that it slips in the hands then that is equally disastrous. The answer is to grip the club firmly in both hands, but not so strongly that the forearm muscles tighten to create tension. Aim for the same degree of pressure you would use to hold and throw a ball.

Fig. 14 'Normal' grip: V pointing between chin and right shoulder.

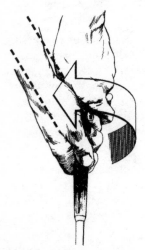

Fig. 15 'Strong' grip: both hands turned too far right, showing four knuckles of left hand.

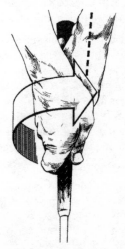

Fig. 16 'Weak' grip: both hands turned too far left, showing no knuckles on left hand.

3

THINK BEFORE
YOU SWING

The fascination of the golf swing has already withstood some 500 years of technical study, and it may well do so for as long again. Expert research has provoked a barrage of countless theories on how best to master the complexities of the swing, and yet ironically nothing could be simpler than its objective. All that is required of it is to deliver the clubface to the ball square to the line of target, and with just the right amount of power to project it the required distance.

As a beginner you do not need to involve yourself in the advanced technicalities of the golf swing, indeed, you should avoid doing so at all cost. Otherwise, you will, as we say, become 'fouled up in the mechanics of the game' and fail to recognise that basically, when approached in the correct manner, golf is essentially a simple challenge. If you restrict your curiosity for a start to gaining a good understanding of the fundamentals of the game, then you will safely build the foundation for a lifetime of enjoyment.

An hour or two spent studying the methods of champions on the course as they play under pressure, answering both the physical and mental challenges of the game at the highest level, offer a priceless lesson without cost. It will also help you to understand that there is no such thing as one perfect golf swing.

While the outstanding players all observe the fundamentals, they have their own individual styles, largely dictated by physique. For example, a player of over six feet will swing the club in a different manner to a golfer of stockier build. So, if you wish to learn by imitation, and many thousands of newcomers do so quite successfully, it is obviously wise to study someone whose physique is similar to your own.

——— Develop a mental picture ———

What should we be looking for when we study a professional on the golf course? For a start, particular note should be taken of how he carefully thinks about the objective of the shot he is about to make before even addressing the ball. The complete golf swing takes only about two seconds, so there really is no time to think during it. The good golfer will develop a *mental picture* of the shot he wants to hit. The object is to put the ball into the easiest position for the next shot, and he will be putting positive thoughts to work to make sure that this is done. A great golf swing is no help unless supported by good course strategy.

Fig. 17

Fig. 18

Addressing the ball

Once having settled on his objective the expert stands to the ball and **addresses** it in a relaxed manner.

The head is cocked slightly to the right so that he is looking at the back of the ball, and it remains steady throughout the entire swing. It is impossible to over-emphasise the importance of keeping the head steady. You must overcome the temptation to watch the clubhead on the takeaway for this leads to a sway and complete loss of balance.

Fig. 19

The backswing

This is a co-ordinated movement of hands, shoulders, hips and legs. The left knee points to a spot behind the ball, the hips turn 45°, the shoulders a full 90° so that the back is now pointing towards the target; the left arm is kept firm and smoothness is the key to the whole

Fig. 20

Fig. 21

movement. There is no snatching of the clubface away from the ball. When the turn is properly completed, then the clubhead will also be aimed at the target.

The downswing

This is triggered by a slight lateral movement of the hips and a pulling down of the arms. Then a lively use of the hands together with a turning of the hips at impact allows the clubface to meet the back of the ball at maximum power. Success does not depend on brute force, but on timing to achieve top speed precisely at impact.

If you think of the golf swing as a gear change in a car then it helps to understand what is wanted. Bottom gear is maintained for a smooth takeaway and after a short pause at the top of the swing the higher gears come into use as acceleration is built up to give the clubhead the power it needs.

Fig. 22

Fig. 23

Fig. 24

All this energy has to be generated smoothly. The expert does not rush, he controls his power. In the beginning, it does no harm to try and swing back and down at the same speed. This will encourage smoothness, and the law of gravity will automatically quicken the downswing for you.

The follow-through

Do not underestimate the importance of the follow-through, for it is just as much a part of the whole co-ordinated exercise as the initial takeaway. The head remains steady, the body balanced, and after keeping the clubface square to the target through the ball, the hands respond to the momentum of the shot and turn over. A really good golf swing leads eventually to a poised and elegant position at the finish.

Fig. 25

Fig. 26

Fig. 27

—— Recognise your limitations ——

It has been claimed often enough, by both the best and the worst of golfers, that the game is more of a mental challenge than a physical test of ability. We believe the two departments to be of equal importance, but accept that the first essential when stepping onto a golf course is to appreciate your own limitations. All too often the average golfer will wreck his score, ruin his day, deny himself a prize, give victory to an opponent, with one careless, ill-conceived shot. All too often he forgets his limitations, and attempts a shot that is not only beyond his own capabilities, but one which would be shunned even by an Open champion as being too adventurous.

Frequently, we see the best of tournament professionals, once having got into serious trouble, playing sideways to reach the safety of the fairway. But it is not uncommon to see the average golfer, faced with a similar problem, attempting a recovery of near miraculous proportions. He feels some compulsion to hit the ball forward, even when there is a virtual forest barring his way. He pays dearly for this bravado and lack of thought. It is absolutely essential to think ahead, visualise the next shot, determine in your mind where you need to hit the ball to make that one easier. Golf strategy, or course management as it is becoming better known, has been likened to a game of chess, each move fitting into a pattern of success. You will never become a good golfer, never even play to a modest handicap with consistency, unless you understand and accept your limitations.

To meet this need you have to be in the right frame of mind from the start, and that means avoiding arriving at the club with no time to spare and having to rush to the first tee. Always allow fifteen minutes at least for a gentle warming up. Why risk three hours of enjoyment on the course for the want of a little practice? Thirty balls with a wedge, gently working up to a full swing, can suffice. A few chips and a little putting will help take away the tension. All the time work on the fundamentals.

Nervousness on the first tee is inevitable if you have no idea what is going to happen when you swing. It is what you deserve if you have not bothered to go to the practice ground and rid yourself of this fear by going through the same process that you will face on the tee. Adopt a drill, follow a set routine, and you will find that it is a great antidote to nerves. Establish a pattern – the same number of practice swings

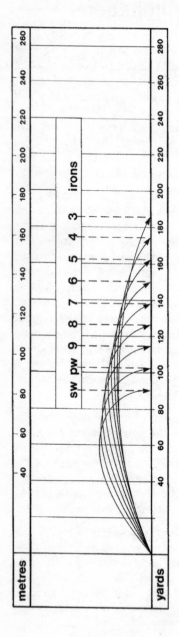

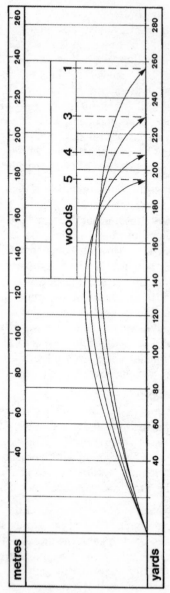

Fig. 28 Yardage chart showing distances possible in helpful conditions for average golfers with woods and irons.

before each shot, the same waggle of the clubhead to release tension, the same time spent addressing the ball before takeaway. This can be especially important.

Consistency and confidence are like the chicken and the egg in posing the question of which comes first. Certainly, good golf cannot be played without them. The one certain thing is that both are bred on the practice ground. Every golfer should know how far he is naturally capable of hitting the ball with each club in the bag and he must develop the consistency to achieve that distance every time. The chart on page 24 shows the normal distances achieved with the different clubs by the average golfer.

4
THE ADDRESS

The correct 'set-up' in golf, a combination of ball position, aim, stance and posture, requires a routine drill which the golfer ignores at his peril. It is the basis for success, or – for those who fail to make a meticulous habit of observing its importance – a certain cause of every conceivable form of bad shot. Quite frequently, on the practice ground at a major tournament, you will see one top professional having his set-up drill checked by another. The very best players invariably recognise its vital bearing in determining how well they perform on the course. Unfortunately, not all average golfers share the same understanding. They will spend hours experimenting with their swings in the search for an answer to a problem when, most likely, the fault lies in the set up and a few seconds is all that is required to determine the answer.

In the set-up position, the golfer is exactly like the marksman sighting his rifle. You must get it right, or miss the target. There is no room for carelessness, or for undue haste in wanting to 'pull the trigger' and hit the ball. Certainly, a few moments more spent in perfecting the address can save five minutes of searching in the woods afterwards. There can be no argument with the fact that the way you set up has a direct bearing on the way you swing the club. Most bad shots are created at the address position long before the swing starts, and the expert professional can estimate with reasonable accuracy the handicap of an amateur merely by watching him stand to the ball. Which leads to one of the truest sayings in golf – there has never yet been a good golfer with a bad set-up, or a really bad golfer with a good set-up.

We will begin with the ball position. The first, best suited to the kind of conditions encountered on most European golf courses, requires the ball to be positioned equidistant between the heels of the feet when playing the short irons, from the number 8 down to the sand wedge. As the clubs lengthen to meet the call for longer shots, so the position of the ball changes. The medium irons, numbers 7, 6 and 5, need the ball to be mid-way between the left heel and the centre of the body. At the same time the feet are gradually being placed wider apart. The long irons, the fairway woods and the driver call for the ball to be opposite or just inside the left heel, and the spacing of your feet will match the width of your shoulders.

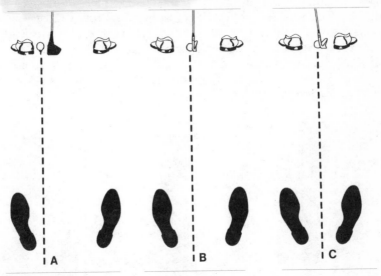

Fig. 29 Ball position at address for:
A Driver, fairway
woods, long irons
B Medium irons
C Short irons

The second method, favoured for golf courses where the grass is in a lush condition, calls for the ball to be played opposite or just inside the left heel for all shots. The feet are placed about six inches apart for the wedge, but while the ball remains in a constant position, the right foot is moved further to the right progressively for the longer clubs, until on reaching the driver, the width is again equal to that of the shoulders.

— Aim with the care of a marksman —

The importance of the aim – the correct alignment of the clubface at the address – must be obvious. Again, it is just like the sharpshooter marksman sighting his rifle onto the bulls-eye of the target. You should take great care to place the clubface behind the ball, square to the line of your intended shot. A good many average golfers mistakenly hurry their way through the process, place the club down in a more or less square position, and trust that some compensation through instinct will correct any error in the downswing. It very rarely does. If as little as a 1° error at the address is maintained throughout the swing, and the ball is hit 200 yards, then it is obvious that it is going to miss the target by a wide margin. The more solidly the ball is struck, the greater the punishment. Only bad golfers set up to the ball with the clubface in a closed (facing left of the target) or open (aimed right of the target) position. You must take care to ensure that the clubface is placed behind the ball, square to the target.

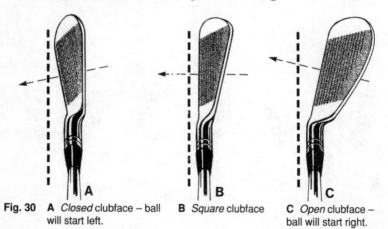

Fig. 30 **A** *Closed* clubface – ball will start left.   **B** *Square* clubface   **C** *Open* clubface – ball will start right.

A common and costly mistake made by many beginners when using irons is to square the top edge of the blade to the ball and line of target. So take care to line up with the *bottom* or *leading edge* of the club. The top edge of the club should point to the right of the target.

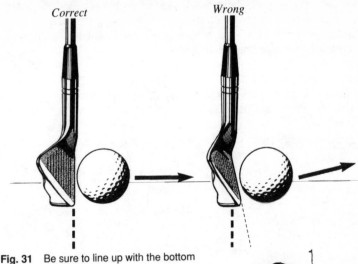

Correct   *Wrong*

Fig. 31 Be sure to line up with the bottom
or leading edge of the clubface square to
the target – *not* the top edge.

To achieve the correct stance and
body alignment demanded for a
square set up it is helpful to imagine
playing golf on a railway line. When
the club is placed behind the ball,
aimed at the target, the feet, knees,
hands, hips and shoulders are all
running parallel to the intended line
of the shot. The left arm and the
shaft of the club need to be in a
reasonably straight line, comfortably
straight for flexibility is essential,
and the right arm has to be slightly
bent with the elbow pointing
towards the front of the right hip.

Fig. 32 To achieve the correct
set-up routine, imagine playing
golf on a railway line.

You should, as you are learning, concentrate on the 'square set up'
approach to golf. There are variations (see Figure 33), but these are
best left alone until you are thoroughly equipped with the fundamental techniques. Then, you can with justification experiment in a great
many directions, for outside of the fundamentals there is nothing

absolutely rigid in golf. There is no one way to play the game. A day at a tournament, spent watching the very best professionals, will make this very plain. It is all a matter of finding out by experiment which variations most help your game.

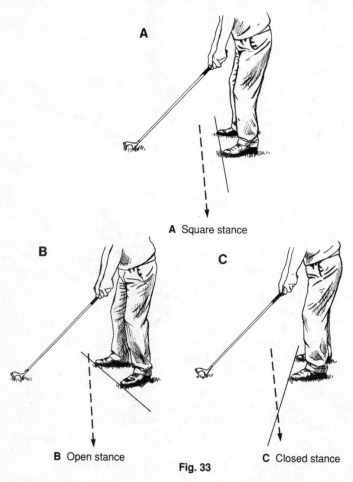

A Square stance

B Open stance   **C** Closed stance

Fig. 33

Golf demands a turning or rotation of the body and free swing of the arms and hands, and for this a good posture is essential. The first requirement is to stand the correct distance from the ball at the address position. The simplest aid to determine this is to stand to the ball, and lower the club until the butt end of the grip touches the left leg about two inches above the knee. Then bend forward from the hips, taking care to keep the back straight. Do not crouch; to become cramped at the address is to deny the hands and arms any chance of swinging freely. Stand proud, hold your head up, do not let your chin drop down onto your chest, as this can only impair the movement of your shoulders, causing them to lift instead of turning on a flat plane. Bad positioning of the head will also prevent a full pivot.

Hold the chin up and the head steady to allow the shoulders to turn freely for a full pivot.

Fig. 34 Incorrect address position.   **Fig. 35** Correct address position.

Your knees should be flexed forward and inwards, and the weight needs to be evenly distributed between your feet for good balance and mobility. Your head position is also extremely important in maintaining a balance. It should, at the address, be behind a line drawn vertically up from the ball, and it should stay there throughout the entire swing (Figure 35). A steady head position is necessary to allow a full, free swing; but 'steady' does not mean holding it rigidly. To be rigid is to create tension, and tension is always an obstacle to good golf. It makes a correct posture, which dictates a golfer's swing plane, quite impossible. So the message to remember is: stand proud to the ball, feel relaxed and comfortable, keep the head behind the ball and steady.

5

THE BACKSWING

As you try to meet the challenge of playing consistently to the limit of your ability, to enjoy the pleasures of the game to the full, you can be greatly helped at any stage by pausing to develop a clear mental picture of the immediate objective. You will find this especially true at the start of the backswing – the all-important takeaway movement based on a rhythmic, balanced, highly co-ordinated and power-generating use of the body. If any one unit –arms, legs, hips, shoulders, head – fails to do its duty, then trouble looms. They must work together like a well-rehearsed relay team. Rather than trying to think of each component part and seriously risk confusion, you will benefit from concentrating on just two primary thoughts. You should start the backswing with the picture of a slowly revolving door in your mind. This will give you a mental image of what you are trying to imitate, and convey a sense of the smoothness and rhythm to be achieved. Then on the completion of the backswing you can visualise your body as a tightly coiled spring held under control and ready to unleash its energy.

A modest waggle of the clubhead or forward press with the hands to relieve tension, starts the backswing. The hands are the great dictators in golf, through them all the muscles of the body are put to work, the clubhead answers to their every command, and so they must be kept active. The takeaway has been called 'the most important eighteen inches in golf' and has prompted a multitude of theories. It is essential in the early stages, however, to simplify your task as much as possible, and you can do this by concentrating on a one-piece movement to waist level. The feeling you have to develop is one of the hands, arms, shoulders and clubhead moving as one unit.

Fig. 36 The backswing turns the body into a powerful coil.

Fig. 37 The first 18 inches of the backswing dictate everything that follows.

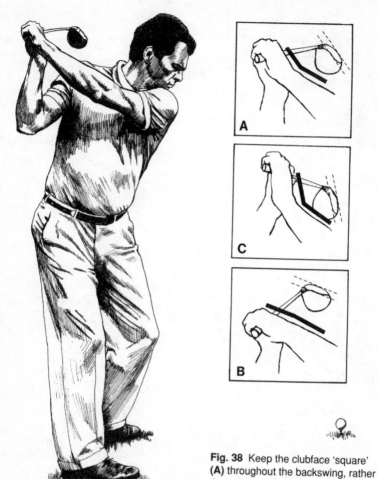

Fig. 38 Keep the clubface 'square' **(A)** throughout the backswing, rather than closed **(B)** or open **(C)**.

When the clubhead is at waist level, the clubface should be 'square' to your body which has started to pivot, and the same number of knuckles on the left hand will be visible as at the address position. While the arms swing around and upwards, the shoulders turn on as flat a plane as possible.

Fig. 39 The club should go no further
than parallel with the ground.

Turn the shoulders on a flat
plane – never tilt them.

Settle for comfort

Many of the requirements of the backswing are supplied by nature. The coiling of the upper part of the body will force the hips to turn through the necessary 45°, and the left knee, helped by a slight raising of the left heel, will co-operate in turn by pointing to a spot behind the ball. Ideally, the pivot continues until a firm left arm has the hands head high, the club shaft parallel to the ground, and the shoulders at 90° so that the back now faces the target. This, it has to be accepted, demands a state of athletic suppleness which is not common to all beginners; so it should be remembered that more harm is done by straining to reach a position that is uncomfortable, than by settling for a restricted swing.

It is still quite possible to play excellent golf with a three-quarter swing and several top tournament professionals have proved this point. Do not make the common mistake of thinking that the clubhead should be taken straight back from the ball, on an extension of the target line, and then brought back to impact point in the same way. The golf swing does not allow this to happen; for it to be possible, your body would have to be bent forward at the address so that your spine was parallel to the ground. The successful golfer must have the image of rounded golf swing, and the mental picture of a revolving door best provides it.

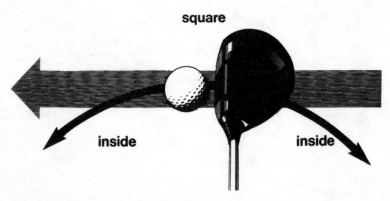

Fig. 40 A good swing delivers the clubhead from the inside to square to the inside again.

Your left arm must be kept as firm as possible throughout the backswing, and as your right arm bends, its elbow should be kept reasonably close to your body. At the top of the backswing, your left shoulder will brush your chin. It cannot be stressed too strongly that throughout the whole of the co-ordinated movement of the body, your head position must remain steady. If the head moves the arc of the swing will change, and when that happens the chances of bringing the clubface back squarely to the ball are remote. During the backswing, your weight is transferred naturally and gradually to the right foot. Do not worry about when and how your wrists should be cocked; nature will take its course and they will behave accordingly.

Fig. 41 For a full drive, 75% of the body weight should be on the inside of the right foot at completion of the backswing.

While there is no one ideal swing plane for all golfers, the position of the clubface at the top of the backswing should be common to all. It should not be too 'open' with the toe pointing towards the ground, or too 'closed' with the clubface towards the sky. The rhythm of the backswing is dictated by two words – slow and smooth. The vast majority of beginners swing far too quickly and very rarely do we see one who does not need to slow down.

Fig. 42(i) Three different positions of the clubhead at the top of the swing: **A** open with the toe pointing towards the ground; **B** closed with the clubface towards the sky; **C** square. You should be square at the top of the swing.

WRONG

WRONG

CORRECT

Fig. 42(ii) Three different alignments of the club shaft at the top of the swing: **A** pointing left of the target; **B** pointing right of the target; and **C** pointing at the target. **C** is correct.

A

WRONG

B

WRONG

C

CORRECT

A persistent problem for those learning the game, and one which you must cure at an early stage, comes from allowing the hips to move to the right with a lateral movement instead of turning during the take-away. Any tendency to sway in this manner can be corrected with another mental picture. Imagine that you are swinging inside a barrel. The only way to avoid scraping the inside is to turn your hips properly.

Fig. 43 To avoid the dangers of swaying, imagine that you are swinging inside a barrel.

Tilting your shoulders instead of turning them on a flat plane is equally harmful. A good practice routine for this department of the game is to stand with your feet together while hitting with medium irons. It compels a correct turning of the body – otherwise loss of balance would cause you to fall off the shot. Remember too that the grip must be kept firm throughout. At the top of the swing you should be gripping the club just as firmly as you were at the address position. A simple practice-ground aid is to place a scorecard between the top joints of the two thumbs. If it falls out during the backswing then the hands are not working together.

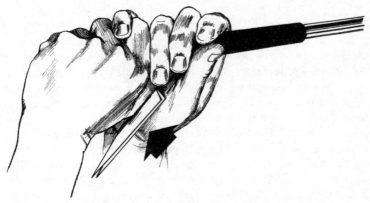

Fig. 44 The left thumb is directly under the shaft at the top of the backswing, and the grip should be just firm enough to hold a scorecard in place as a practice-ground exercise.

6

THE DOWNSWING AND FOLLOW-THROUGH

Scientists who study the physical demands of golf with the use of sophisticated robots and timing devices can make the playing of the game seem a daunting affair. They delight in proving that once the golfer has recognised the need for a momentary pause at the top of the backswing, and then committed himself to attacking the ball, he has only one-fifth of a second to get it all right by delivering the clubface at a speed of some 100 miles per hour to a precisely square point of impact. In effect, however, the downswing is a simple matter, which calls for the observance of a basic drill in order to allow nature to take its course through a succession of reflex actions.

The first essential of the drill is to understand clearly the principles of the 'inside to out, and then inside again' arc of the downswing. Obviously, at the top of the swing the clubhead is inside the line to the target, having been taken to that position by the pivoting of the body. Now the challenge is to return the clubface to the ball on the same line as the backswing, and in such a manner that at the exact moment of impact it will be square, thus precisely duplicating its position at the point of address. Then if the right balance is maintained, the controlled momentum of the swing will carry the clubhead back inside the line for the follow-through to complete the in-to-in arc of the swing (see Figure 45).

A brief pause at the top before starting the process of attacking the ball, is helpful. It is a safeguard against 'starting down' before completing the backswing properly. Failure to complete a full pivot is

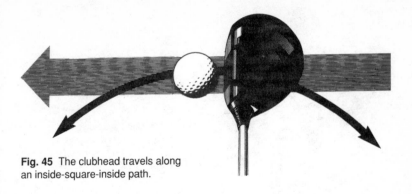

Fig. 45 The clubhead travels along an inside-square-inside path.

one of the most persistent problems for beginners. Any curtailing of the shoulder turn on the way back will encourage the clubhead to be taken back on an outside arc resulting in an out-to-in swing path with the clubface cutting across the ball and creating all kinds of trouble. Golf then becomes an awfully difficult game, whereas the correct positioning of the body at the top of the swing makes the rest so much simpler.

The one-fifth of a second it takes to reach the point of impact allows only one constructive swing thought. We suggest that this should be concerned with starting the downswing with as light lateral movement of the hips – a slide of about six centimetres to the left, parallel to the target line, and a tugging down of the arms. Done properly, this movement works like a key in unlocking the rest of the body from its fully coiled state at the top. It sets the correct angle of attack, and initiates the transfer of weight back to the left side. Trying to think of all the component parts of the downswing is to invite disaster. Concentrate on getting the first initial hip movement right and a fair degree of 'auto pilot' will take over. As your arms and hands pull down together with the shifting of your hips, the coil unwinds. After the slide, your hips begin to turn, so establishing the inside arc of the downswing. The hips and arms are the leaders in the downswing, everything else follows to their command. This combination is a safeguard against your right shoulder throwing the club across the line. 'Hitting from the top' as it is sometimes mistakenly called guarantees the clubhead approaching the ball from across the target line.

Fig. 46 A slight sideways thrust of the hips triggers the downswing with a downward pull of the arms ...

Fig. 47 ... and guides the way to the correct position at impact. The weight is transferred to the left side of the body, hips now turned, head still steady behind the ball and clubface square to the target.

You must resist the urge to attack the ball from the top of the swing with the upper body only. Unfortunately, it is a very easy trap to fall into, often stemming from an obsession with 'power', trying to hit the ball a maximum distance, which may mislead you into throwing your right shoulder into the action instead of starting the whole downward movement with a slight lateral shift of the hips and then co-ordinated turning of the hips and free swing of the arms. There is no sense in achieving a good, smooth backswing and then lunging at the ball. While creating energy, the downswing also has to be controlled, balanced, and geared to a rhythm that will allow maximum power to be reached at the point of impact. Essential to this is keeping the head back behind the ball until well after impact. Unnecessary movement of the head is the first step towards swaying, and will inevitably ruin your swing.

Fig. 48 The head must stay behind the ball throughout the swing.

Allow nature to help

As in the backswing, do not become obsessed with thinking about when and how to un-cock the wrists. Let nature take care of it for a start, any little refinements in the search for added power can be taken care of at a later stage. At this point, you should restrict yourself to doing what is simplest. You will come to no harm by concentrating upon the thought that your hands do not begin to unleash the power in the downswing until they have come into what is called the hitting area, the last third of the downward arc. The primary object is to create a swing of gradual acceleration, timed to reach maximum velocity at the moment of impact.

Again, it can be extremely helpful to study a top tournament professional. Notice how he will seemingly hit the ball with half the explosive energy used by the average golfer – and yet send it half as far again.

The ultimate objective is to swing the clubhead *through* the ball and to achieve this it is helpful to think of swinging the clubhead down the target line for a couple of feet after impact. This is not literally possible, of course – the turning of the body so that the chest is facing the target, or even slightly left of it, must bring the clubhead back inside the line. But it is a thought process, and another mental picture, that encourages good timing of the shot. You may understandably question the importance of the follow-through, on the grounds that once you have hit the ball and sent it on its way to the target, there is nothing you can do to influence the path of its flight. But you will soon learn that what comes after impact has a real meaning on the golf swing. A stylish, balanced finish with the arms extended through the ball for the hands to finish high, and with the left side of the body bearing all the weight, becomes a meaningful judgement of all the good that has been done before. The basic drills of the downswing have to be observed and carried out if the follow-through is to be successfully completed. Once impact has been achieved, the 'down, under and through' process of the shoulders continues as the body rotates, the right hand climbs over the left at the limit of extension, the right knee continues to move in towards the left, the head, held steady for so long, is at last allowed to come up with the arms, and if the balance is right, the process of gradual deceleration will lead to a neat and tidy finish. Then, hopefully, comes the time to enjoy the satisfaction of a well-struck shot that has resulted from a successful appreciation that good golf is dependent upon a rhythmic swinging of the arms, and a balanced transference of weight.

Fig. 49 Good balance must be maintained for a poised finish to the swing.

Fig. 50 Swing the clubhead *through* the ball, and then let the hands roll over naturally.

GOLF

Fig. 51 The good golfer at his best can come close to the perfection of the robot.

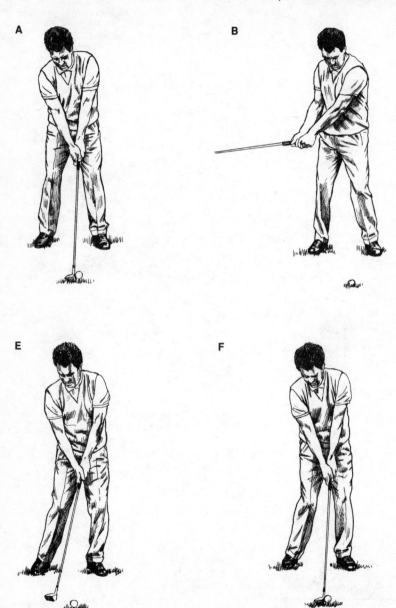

A

B

E

F

— 48 —

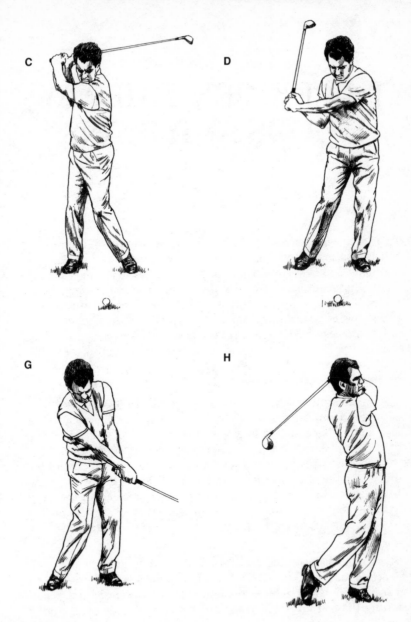

7

THE DRIVER, FAIRWAY WOODS AND IRONS

There is no question about which shot consistently offers the greatest satisfaction in golf; nothing can compare with the pleasure of hitting a straight and powerful drive from the tee. But the beginner's quest for this ultimate enjoyment requires a sound understanding of the basic techniques involved. Otherwise, initial failures can swiftly lead to a feeling of intimidation, and the tee is essentially a place for confidence, not negative thoughts. It is common to hear a golfer complain that he has always been a poor, or at best, indifferent driver of the ball. Those who fail to learn well at the start inevitably develop bad habits which become increasingly difficult to cure.

The first requirement is to show the driver itself the respect it deserves. A combination of straight face – usually 11° in loft – and long shaft – the standard length is forty-three inches – makes it the most difficult club to master. On the other hand, however, there is the compensation of being able to put the ball on a tee peg for a perfect lie every time the driver is used from the tee. Even so, it is wise for the beginner to accept that the driver can create problems in the early learning stages. No satisfaction can be gained by using it to hit the ball a prodigious distance, if it is then lost in trees either side of the fairway.

There is no disgrace, but considerable wisdom, in first gaining confidence on the tee by using a No. 3 wood, sometimes still referred to as a spoon, which has a clubface loft of around 14°. Obviously, this makes hitting the ball up and into the air much easier. The concession of something like 30 yards in distance is a small sacrifice to make for the reward of accuracy. When consistency has been achieved this way, then the driver can be tackled with confidence.

The first step in developing a good driving technique is to make sure to *tee up* the ball properly. It should be placed on the tee peg at a height that ensures half the ball showing above the face of the driver at the address position, and as already explained, it should be approximately in line with the left heel. A slight variation is permissible to meet personal needs. For example, if you tend to slice, you may find it helpful to move the ball back an inch or so.

Fig. 52 The correct height for teeing up the ball for a drive.

Fig. 53 The correct teeing-up position.

The swing demanded by the use of the driver is simply the basic swing. But because of the power and distance factors involved, strict observance of the fundamentals is never more important. Rhythm and clubhead speed are the critical requirements, and this is the time to be aware of the fact that power is not so much about hitting the ball hard, but striking it well. Beware the temptation to strain for extra momentum by rushing the swing. The need, now more than ever, is to swing smoothly, making the fullest possible pivot, transferring seventy-five per cent of the weight to the right side on the backswing and then back to the left on the way down, and only then speeding the hands through the impact zone. The objective is to have the clubface make contact with the ball slightly on the upswing with a sweeping action. The drive with a wood club has to be a sweep, unlike that with the irons which calls for a slightly downward angle of attack.

Fig. 54 The driver must make square contact with the ball at the start of the upswing ...

... while the irons strike the ball on the downswing, thus achieving greater backspin.

The whole secret of good driving is to have a mental picture of the clubhead sweeping the ball off the tee peg to fly high. But while observing the demands of technique, do not overlook the strategy that has to be applied to every drive. The primary aim is to hit the ball from the tee to a position on the fairway that makes the next shot towards the green as simple as possible.

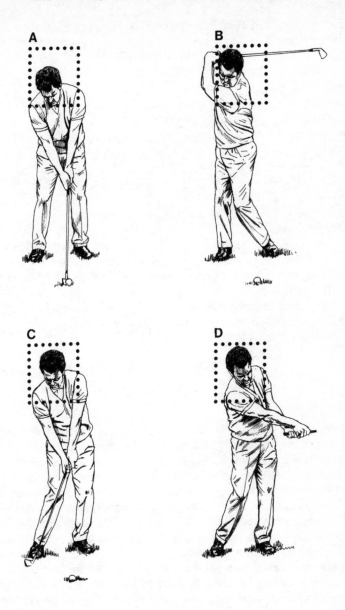

Fig. 55 Keep the head steady throughout the swing.

The fairway woods – think 'smooth'

The ability to consistently play good fairway wood shots rests largely on allowing the loft of the clubface to do the work for which it has been designed. You must overcome any urge to try and scoop the ball into the air. Once again, all you have to do is to sweep the clubhead through the impact zone and allow the loft of each club to work. More than ever, the mental picture has to be of a smooth, slow start to the backswing, keeping the clubhead low to the ground for the first 18 inches or so. Keep thinking 'smooth', for the fairway wood shot is a sweeping action, not an aggressive attacking of the ball. Remember, there is *no substitute for accuracy* in golf. Ideally, the ball position for fairway wood shots is just inside the left heel. But when faced with a poor lie, moving it back an inch or two towards the centre of the stance can help. While enjoying that amount of freedom of choice, be sure to observe religiously the basic laws – swing smoothly, make a full pivot, sweep through with balance and rhythm, and never force it. A controlled swing is of paramount importance when using the fairway wood.

The long irons – aim for a 'pinching' effect

Iron play is essentially about accuracy, but the first lesson to be learned has to do with distance. Good scoring will always be dependent upon successful club selection, and the importance of this facet of the game has been recognised to the extent that no top tournament professional is likely to go on the course without his yardage chart. The beginner also has to know the maximum distance he can hit with each iron. Such knowledge automatically builds consistency and confidence into his game. It is very difficult indeed to concentrate on making a sound swing if the mind is filled with doubt about whether the right club had been chosen for the task. Playing the long irons, Nos 2, 3, and 4 – with clubface lofts ranging from 20° to 27° – will give you more problems than any other area of the game. You would be wise for a start to leave the No 2 iron well alone for it demands a degree of expertise that can only come with experience. To begin with, an understanding is required of the main difference between hitting the tee shot and an iron. The drive, as we have explained, calls for the ball to be swept into the air as the clubhead starts upwards. But the purpose of the iron shot is to make a downward contact – the clubface striking the ball first and then the turf in front of it just as it reaches the lowest point in the arc of its downswing. A 'pinching' effect is created and the loft of the club imparts backspin on the ball and this in turn helps it to 'brake' to a halt on coming to earth. The need to hit down should not be allowed to develop into a chopping swing, however. The same basic principles apply in general to long irons as for the woods.

The ball should be positioned a shade inside the left heel and the feet must be comfortably far enough apart to provide the solid base needed for a successful partnership between balance and power. The requirement is to hit down on the back of the ball and to help this, your hands must be slightly ahead of the ball at the point of address. At impact, this position will be duplicated, the hands leading the clubhead as part of the more pronounced down-and-through swing pattern essential for iron shots. Swing well within yourself, concentrating on rhythm. Never try to scoop the ball; always have confidence that the loft of the club will get the ball airborne.

The medium irons – use the power of positive thinking

So often, the medium irons are the making or the breaking of a good score. They offer the accuracy needed to attack with confidence. To make the most of the opportunity a routine becomes necessary. Establish a set pattern, make a habit of creating a mental picture of the shot that is needed before addressing the ball. The power of positive thinking is sometimes stronger than the physical strength of the body muscles. When you are clear in your mind about what is wanted, then stand to the ball, pick a spot a few inches in front of it – a weed, an old divot mark, or whatever – that is on the target line and use this as an aiming aid for making sure that the clubface is set square. If you go through this procedure each time, knowing how far it is to the target and that you have selected the right club, then the anxiety is taken out of the shot.

The short irons – hit firmly and cleanly

The key factor with playing the short irons is, of course, accuracy and it is obvious that if you are ambitious to improve your game and reduce your score you can best do so by saving strokes on and around the green. The satisfaction of learning to drive well should not be at the expense of practising with the short irons. Accurate pitching with the Nos 8 and 9 irons, the wedge and sand wedge, call for standing a little nearer to the ball, and with the feet closer together. The ball should be positioned equidistant between the feet. Make sure the knees are flexed for balance, and concentrate on a three-quarter swing; but still be sure to make a full turn of the body, and hit through the ball. It is one thing to restrict the swing, quite another to quit on the shot. The art of successful short iron play is to hit the ball firmly and cleanly, taking the divot after it has been sent on its way. As ever, all the basic fundamentals of the golf swing, beginning with the need to keep the head steady throughout, still apply.

8

THE SHORT PITCH
AND CHIP SHOTS

The development of an effective short game – basically the ability to hole the ball in two shots from thirty yards or so off the green – is one of golf's easier challenges. Success can come rapidly with practice for the fundamentals involved are quite simple, and the rewards encourage dedication. The anguish of a poor drive or wayward iron approach is soon forgotten when the threat of a wasted stroke is overcome with a precisely judged chip or pitch and single putt. Better still is the feeling of 'getting down in two' for a birdie. Tournament professionals expect to do this as a matter of course, and there is no reason why the average amateur should not improve his scores by developing the technique and 'touch' required for a useful short game.

First we need to be clear about the difference between the short pitch, usually played with the 9 iron, the wedge, or sand wedge, and the chip shot, best tackled with something like a No 7 iron. Different situations will dictate which method and club is wanted. The chip is generally regarded as a shot of low trajectory that causes the ball to roll a fair distance after landing on the green. But the short-game pitch is a high, floating shot, played with plenty of back-spin so that it bites, and the ball stops quickly on landing upon the green. Obviously, if a hazard of any kind, a bunker or a stream for example, stands between the ball and the green, then a pitch becomes necessary. If, however, a straightforward shot to the flag stick is offered, then the chip may well be the most suitable method.

The chip shot

The stance for the chip shot should be slightly open – the left foot
withdrawn some six inches behind the right. By doing this, you will
be partially facing the target and with the feet only six inches apart it
helps to swing the club slightly outside the line. The ball is positioned
mid-way between the feet. Be sure to grip the club about three inches
from the end of the shaft, what we call 'choking down' on the club.
This will bring the ball closer to the body and sharpen the 'feel' that
ultimately separates success and failure. The distance of the shot
decides the length of the backswing, a half swing is usually enough –
what we do not want at any cost is a long swing and deceleration on
the way down in an attempt to soften the impact.

Fig. 56 The arms and club
shaft form a Y when set-up is
right for the chip shot.

SEVERIANO BALLESTEROS fearless and natural

NICK FALDO determination and dedication

JACK NICKLAUS success beyond compare

JOHN DALY seeing is believing

GREG NORMAN flying to the top of the world

ERNIE ELS the burden of fame

BERNHARD **L**ANGER **champion pioneer**

FRED COUPLES calm and cool winner

Body movement must be restricted to an absolute minimum, the mental picture needed for the chip needs to be of a hands-and-arms swing. The object is to flight the ball onto the green, covering a third of the distance to the flag stick, and then to let it run the rest of the way. So a low, punched shot with restricted follow-though is demanded, and for this the wrists have to be kept fairly firm throughout the crisp, but smooth stroke. There is never a more important moment for keeping the head steady. The more delicate the shot the greater need there is for balance.

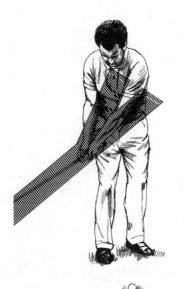

Fig. 57 The wrists are kept firm and the Y maintained for restricted backswing.

Fig. 58 Swing the Y as a one-piece unit through the ball.

The pitch

The short pitch calls for a successful combination of club and wrist action. The 52° loft of the wedge is usually sufficient and if not there is always the sand iron, 58°, though this rounded sole takes more practice to master. The basics are much the same as for the chip shot. Stand slightly open with the body turned towards the target, and address the ball off the middle of the stance. Pick the spot where you want the ball to land and imprint it on the mind for a clear mental picture. Instead of keeping the wrists firm as in the chip shot, put them to work. Let them punch the clubface in to the back of the ball with authority. It has to be a very definite 'hit down and through' shot every time. Do not scoop, have strong positive thoughts about extending the clubhead through the ball to waist height in the follow-through.

Fig. 59 Address position and three-quarter swing for short-iron accuracy.

Really, there is nothing very difficult about rolling 'three shots into two' as the tournament professionals call it. The key is not to be over-whelmed by the thought that only a short distance has to be covered – still hit the ball firmly.

Fig. 60 To loft the ball high with a short pitch, open the stance and this will assist taking the club back outside the line.

9

BUNKER SHOTS

One of the ironies of golf is that potentially the easiest shot in the game – the recovery from a *green-side sand bunker* – intimidates many players, and certainly all beginners, more than any other. Yet it is the only shot which in normal conditions actually calls for missing the ball. The basic, and extremely simple, objective is to use the club to 'explode' a small quantity of sand out of the bunker in such a way that it carries the ball with it to the green. The cardinal rule is to stay relaxed, but it is all too easy to turn negative thoughts into apprehension, and consequently tension. Certainly, the bunker shot needs to be respected, but never feared.

The overriding objective is, of course, to escape from the bunker at first attempt. There are few more demoralising experiences than taking two or more shots to recover from the sand. So, if the ball is positioned under the steep face of a bunker, making a forward shot in the general direction of the flag stick a risky business, then stop and think of a safer route. There is no shame in playing sideways to escape from a bunker.

As a general rule, never try to take the ball clean from the sand, i.e. you should not try to create a direct impact between clubface and ball as in a normal fairway iron shot. Use the club designed for the job, the sand wedge, and concentrate on having the ball fly out of the bunker on a cushion of sand. The normal green-side bunker shot requires an open clubface to strike the sand an inch or two behind the

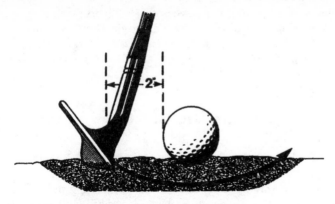

Fig. 61 The basic explosion shot with open clubface.

ball – the margin varies according to the distance of the shot to be hit – and to bounce through the sand at a depth of about an inch. In effect, this is like picking the sand up on a shovel, and hurling it forwards. The ball, sitting on top of the sand, will become part of the whole operation. So the mental image for this shot has to be of the ball taking a ride to the green on a 'divot' of sand.

Fig. 62 Dig both feet down into the sand for a solid base at the right level, to enable the arc of the swing to be lower than the ball.

The preparations begin with the 'digging in' of your feet; the importance of this is to make sure that the base of the stance is an inch or so below the level of the ball. Then, with a normal swing, it becomes easy to have the clubhead ride under the ball. Do not forget that it is important to complete the follow-through, as this will help you keep your shot smooth and authoritative.

Attack the sand

Once the feet have been firmly embedded the ball should be addressed opposite the left heel with the stance open. The clubface must be held open throughout a natural out-to-in swing path. The apprehension felt by the average golfer towards bunker play leads all too often to a timid approach. More than anything, aggression is wanted. Maintain a smooth rhythm, but be sure to attack the sand. Keep body movement to a minimum, and make your hands and arms do the work.

Occasionally, this basic technique has to be varied to meet different circumstances. If the sand is exceptionally hard, or the ball is half buried, then use a closed-face sand iron or even pitching wedge, in order for the leading edge of the club to knife under the ball. But still be sure to aim two inches behind as normal.

The cardinal rule governing *fairway bunker* shots is not to be greedy. Boldness must be tempered with caution. Care has to be taken in the selection of the right club. A perfectly struck shot which flies into the face of the bunker is not bad luck – it's bad thinking. Although you do want to hit your recovery shot the maximum distance, it is worth remembering that the primary objective when in a bunker is to get out at first attempt. The drill for recovering from a fairway bunker begins with wriggling the feet into the sand for a firm foundation. Address the ball from the centre of a square stance, and keep looking at the top of the ball as this encourages a clean strike. Grip firmly to guard against the clubface being turned off line, and concentrate on an active leg action. Above all, think positively, accept that becoming a good bunker player is only a matter of practice. There is absolutely no need to be intimidated by sand.

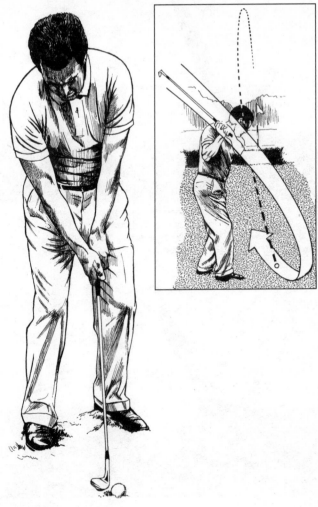

Fig. 63 Remember:
- ball opposite left heel
- open stance and body
- 60% of weight on left leg
- open clubface throughout the swing
- aim two inches behind the ball.

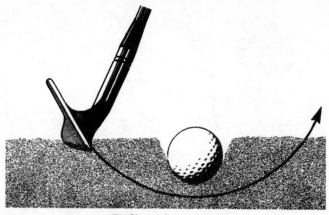

(i) Close the clubface and use a full-power swing to dig the ball out of a buried lie.

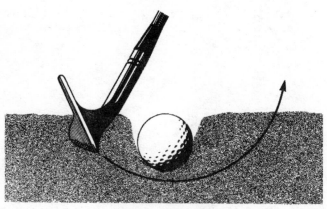

(ii) Use a pitching wedge or closed-face sand iron for a very deeply buried lie, as the sharper edge knifes into the sand.

(iii) Use a strong, down-ward, chopping blow to escape from the 'fried egg' lie.

Fig. 64 Bad lies in bunkers.

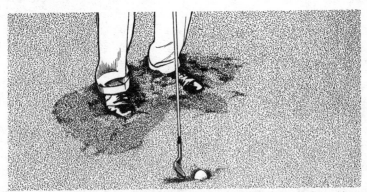

Fig. 65 Dig the feet well into the sand, and use shut clubface, for dealing with a ball buried in a bunker.

10

THE ART OF PUTTING

If there is such a thing as a short cut to lower scores in golf then it is by the putting route. Only one statistic is needed to explain why. The putter is far and away the most used club in the bag – thirty-six times on average for the regulation 18 holes. Therefore, it must offer the greatest opportunity for saving shots through improvement. Tournament professionals recognise this fact by practising their putting for many more hours than any other department of the game. Consequently, the best among them will average 28 to 30 putts a round over an entire season.

Consistently good putting depends upon confidence, and this in turn requires the development of two, equally important, basic skills. A reliable, habitual or 'repeating' stroke that works under pressure is wanted, along with the ability to 'read' the contours and the speed of different greens. Putting has long been accepted as a game within a game, and there are literally hundreds of conflicting methods. Occasionally, the beginner will discover a natural instinct that will make him the envy of far more accomplished golfers. More likely how-ever, you will need to school yourself in the fundamentals of putting, and then use these as the foundation on which to experiment and decide which slight variations best suit. Even then you will soon learn that what works one day can bring nothing but disappointment the next, and there will be no end to the process of experimentation. For inside golf, putting is a law unto itself. There is no one way to putt well, and a day of watching the tournament professionals gives ample proof of this fact. They all have their different styles, and they will always be seen crowding the practice green, testing more and more variations in a never-ending search for improvement.

However fickle putting may be, the fundamentals involved remain firm. The first requirement is to start building confidence by adopting a grip that is comfortable. Most good putters favour what we call the *reverse overlap* – the same principle of thumbs down the shaft, the back of the left hand and the palm of the right hand facing the target, but with the left index finger this time riding over the little finger of the right hand. To putt well, the hands have to work as a unit, and with a delicate sense of 'feel'. The reverse overlap is recommended to the beginner because it is most likely to meet both needs, but that is not to say that other methods are without merit. Extreme variations, such as holding the putter with the hands separated and the left below the right, have been known to win championships. It is all a matter of personal preference. What works for you has to be the best.

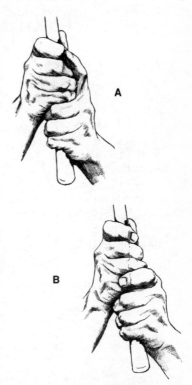

Fig. 66 Two variations of the 'reverse overlap'. Putting grip **A** is the most popular.

There can be no argument, however, about the absolute necessity to keep tension out of the putting stroke. Otherwise the door is opened to creating the dreaded 'yips' – uncontrolled stabbing at the ball instead of a smooth strike and this is usually an extremely difficult affliction to cure. Prevention is much simpler.

To begin, stand to the ball in a completely comfortable manner. The slightest degree of strain is guaranteed to wreck a good putting stroke. Let your arms hang loosely, grip the club firmly but still leaving a light sensitive touch in your fingers, and position your head directly over the ball which is addressed off the inside of the left heel. Your feet and the hips should be slightly open at the address.

Fig. 67 Hold the head steady, directly above the ball.

Now we have established a set-up that allows a mental picture of swinging the putter like a pendulum. This is done by ensuring that the shoulders, arms and hands work as a single component. The object is to form them into a perfect triangle which will rock backwards and forwards.

Fig. 68 The 'rocking triangle' principle for putting: slightly open stance ... head steady ...

It was fashionable in the past to have the hands dominate the stroke, and there were players who enjoyed tremendous success with a wristy method. The 'triangle' influence is now dominant in the modern game. The 'feel' in the hands is rarely the same two days in succession, and so making them the all-governing factor is likely to encourage an inconsistent putting stroke. The responsibility is too much for the hands alone. The answer is to let the 'triangle' formation of the arms and shoulders do the work together. They need a solid base on which to operate, and this is best achieved with the feet about nine inches apart, the knees flexed forwards and inwards, the weight evenly distributed, and the body held still throughout the stroke. Keep the clubhead as low as possible on the backswing and low again on the follow-through after a firm, positive, striking of the ball. Concentrate on maintaining the triangle and making a good strike.

Fig. 69 ... hit through the ball ... be positive ...

Fig. 70 ... same length for follow-through as for backswing.

Always adopt a positive, even an aggressive attitude; this will help you to hole many more putts than those who are so timid that they constantly leave the ball short of the hole. There is nothing like making a bold putt for building up confidence, and there is nothing like confidence for helping you to do it again. So much to do with the art of putting is in the mind – shun negative tactics like the plague.

The development of a sound and repeating putting stroke is no good, however, without the ability to 'read' a green. The art of reading the pace of a green does not come easily. Indeed, the very best of tournament professionals can on occasions, more especially early in a round as they adjust to conditions, be seen committing an error of judgement by putting the ball well past the hole – 'being strong' – or leaving it short, known as 'being weak'. Rarely, however, do they repeat the same mistake. They quickly learn from every lapse, and it is equally important for you to do so as a means of improving. The terms 'fast' and 'slow' greens have obvious definitions. Championship and major tournament venues generally favour, weather and other circumstances permitting, the preparation of fast greens which encourage a smooth, swift rolling of the ball from a delicate use of the putter. The faster the green, within reason, the sterner the examination of a player's skills, and not just with the putter. A fast green places a high premium on the accuracy of approach shots. There is always a 'right' and a 'wrong' spot to place the ball. Twenty feet above the hole, creating the daunting prospect of the first putt sending the ball sliding past the hole to keep rolling downhill as far again, is definitely the 'wrong' place. Top golfers are always careful to reduce the threat of fast greens by hitting their approach shots as close as possible below the hole, so leaving an uphill putt and the chance to attack. Many factors are involved in the preparation of fast greens: weather, soil, drainage, fine grasses, and always the expertise of the greenkeeper with his mower blades set far lower than your lawn at home could withstand. Seaside courses, helped by sandy soil and drying winds, are best suited to really fast greens. In contrast, parkland courses where the soil can be heavy and the grasses require considerable watering, generally have slower greens which demand a much bolder putting stroke. The tendency then is to leave putts short of the hole.

The degree to which a green is fast or slow is mostly a matter of 'feel' for the golfer. But there are ways that you can help yourself. Always learn from an opponent or partner who putts first. Also, drill yourself into the habit of always spending a few minutes on the practice putting green before going to the first tee. There is nothing more damaging to your confidence than the experience of taking three putts at the opening hole after being surprised by the pace of the green. It can help on fast greens to use a light blade putter for a more delicate touch. Or if the greens are extremely lush and slow, try a putter with a heavy head. Remember, every problem in golf has an answer.

11
TROUBLE SHOTS

The enjoyment of playing golf is dependent upon acceptance of the axiom that to err is only human; the perfect golfer will always be a figment of the imagination. Even Open champions rarely claim the satisfaction of hitting more than five or six shots of 100 per cent quality in a single round. Trouble, and escaping from it, is very much an integral part of the game for players of all standards. So learning to cope with the inevitable problems of golf is an essential part of your basic golfing education. The difference between good and bad golfers is never more marked than when they are confronted with trouble.

Beginners frequently share a compulsive urge to attack their problem as quickly as possible. Do not be obsessed with the need to 'get it over with', as this leads to an unthinking assault upon the ball. The result, often as not, is the replacing of one problem with another. Try instead to approach trouble in quite the opposite manner: always take time to study a dilemma on the course with the concentration of a chess player deciding on his next complicated move. Let the rule, *Think it out*, govern your approach, as there is always more than one solution to a problem, and haste certainly does not allow them all to be carefully considered. Remember, too, that there is no law in golf which compels the ball to be hit forward. Sometimes, hitting the ball to the side, or even away from the hole, offers the best escape route from a worrying situation. You should never be too proud to cut your losses in this way. Always play within your own limits; do not press on regardless and hope for a miracle.

When faced with trouble, 80 per cent of the solution lies in the mind. When the solution is desperately serious, do not overlook, as so many beginners do, the simplest solution of all – take advantage of the rules of golf, pick the ball up, and carry it to the best point of safety allowed at the cost of one penalty shot. This can be a lot less expensive than thrashing away wildly in the trees. 'Trouble' shots are an everyday part of golf, and the technique needed to successfully meet their challenge can be mastered with practice.

Uphill lie (Figure 71)

As with all shots that do not allow a level stance, maintaining a proper *balance* throughout the swing is a problem when faced with an uphill lie. Take care to stand perpendicular to the slope, address the ball closer to the left foot than usual, and – because it is obviously going to fly high – take a club one grade stronger than you would normally use for the distance to be covered (a 5 iron instead of a 6, for example).

The gradient will add more weight to the *right* side of the body, making it more difficult to keep clear of the *left* side of the body in the downswing. This will encourage the hands to become more active, and so there will be a tendency to hit the ball to the left. So begin compensating at the address position by aiming a little right of the target.

Downhill lie (Figure 72)

Any problem shot puts an added importance on maintaining a good *rhythm*, so be sure to swing smoothly. Address the ball more towards the right foot, pick the clubhead up a little more quickly with earlier wrist action to counteract the slope, and concentrate on a really solid *down-and-through* impact following the contour of the slope for as long as possible. Guard against swaying and falling forward in the shot, and this time aim off a shade to the left. The natural tendency will be to hit the ball with a *fade* or left-to-right flight. Obviously, the trajectory of the ball is going to be lower. This makes a club with more loft advisable, a 7 iron instead of a 6 iron, for example, according to the distance of the shot.

Fig. 71 The uphill lie encourages the ball to fly left.

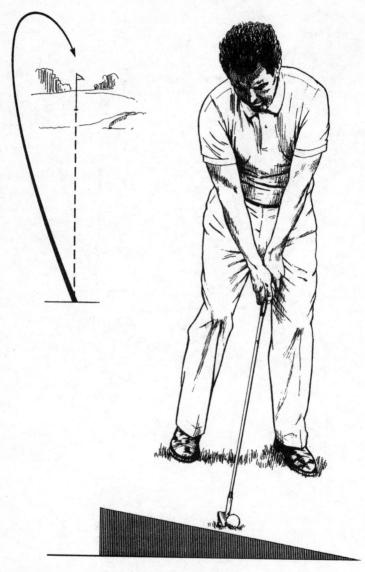

Fig. 72 Allow for a fade or slice from a downhill lie.

—— Side hill lie – ball below feet ——

The left-to-right flight of a slice now becomes the danger, because of the need to stand closer to the ball and adopt an *upright* swing. Aim slightly left, therefore, flex the knees more than usual, keep the weight on the heels, address the ball towards the left foot, grip the club at full length, keep the head steady to help balance, and play the shot with hands and arms.

—— Side hill lie – ball above feet ——

Take a slightly shorter grip of the club –choke down two or three centimetres – to compensate for the flatter swing this situation compels. Keep the weight on the front of the feet to offset the tendency to fall back off balance during the swing. The need to stand further away from the ball, and swing more round the body creates the danger of a right-to-left shot. Allow for this by aiming to the right of the target.

Fig. 73 A When played from below the feet, the ball tends to take a left-to-right flight.

B From above the feet, the ball will tend to hook.

Ball buried in bunker

First, forget heroics, and settle for just getting it safely out of the hazard. Turn the toe of the sand wedge in slightly to *close the club-face* at address, and this will ensure that the leading edge, rather than the flange, will first make contact with the sand at impact. The object is to 'knife' *under the ball and through the sand.* Address the ball towards the right foot and hit down sharply. Go *right through* with the shot: whatever you do, do not become a victim of the most common of all bunker play faults by quitting at impact. Lead with the hands, and put plenty of energy to work.

Fig. 74 When the ball is buried, close the clubface and use the leading edge like a knife, to hit down, under and through with plenty of aggression. The follow-through is important.

Intentional slice

Trees and other obstacles have a nasty habit of blocking the golfer's target line. So learning to 'bend' a ball, as opposed to hitting it straight, can prove extremely helpful on occasions. When the ball has to be hit on a left to right path, then a fade, or more pronounced slice, is wanted. Firstly, remember that it is the *open set-up*, and the *outside-to-in swing path* with an open clubface, that produces the intentional slice. Pick a spot left of the target as the point of aim, and address the ball towards the front of a narrow, open stance.

Fig. 75 An intentional slice can get you out of trouble.

Use the normal grip but with the clubface 'open' or, more precisely, lofted. Select a stronger club than normal, because both the 'bending' of the ball and the need for a restricted three-quarter swing will cause loss of distance. Contrary to everything that has been said before, in this shot the clubhead has to be taken outside the target line on the backswing. Then the outside-to-in path of the downswing will cause the clubface to cut across the ball at impact. The faster the hand action, the more the side-spin imparted on the ball. You will not master this shot without considerable practice, so do not be too ambitious.

Fig. 76 A Open stance for slice.   **B** Closed stance for hook.

Intentional hook

Drop down a club or two – a 6 or 7 iron instead of a 5 – for this shot because a hook causes the ball to run further. Again, use the normal grip, but with the clubface 'closed' or more precisely, 'delofted'. Also close the stance by pulling the right foot back behind the left, aim right of the target, and concentrate on swinging on an *inside-to-out* path with closed clubface. Whip the hands through the shot, let them roll over, and watch the ball fly from right to left.

Fig. 77 Use a more lofted club for the intentional hook, and allow the hands to roll over.

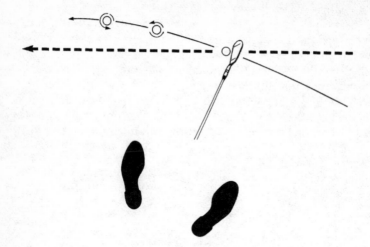

Fig. 78 To hook – close stance, aim right of the target, and whip the hands through the shot with an in-to-out swing.

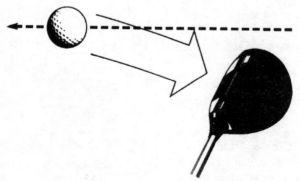

Fig. 79 A Use the normal grip for an intentional hook, close or de-loft the clubface, and remember that the right-to-left flight of the ball will cause it to run further.

B Take the club back inside the line to hook.

Heavy rough

The main danger here is an excess of ambition. Accept that the primary objective has to be getting the ball back into play with one shot. So settle for the club that will do the job with the greatest degree of safety. Play the ball off the middle of the stance, choke down on the club to encourage a *compact swing*, pick the club up sharply and hit *down* and *through* with a slightly open face. Remember that there will be a strong cushion of grass between the clubface and the ball at impact, so backspin will be minimal, if there is any at all. The more likely result is a low trajectory 'flyer' with overspin, causing the ball to run further than usual. This cushion of grass will also close the clubface at impact so take care to address the ball with the face slightly open, pointing to the right of the target.

Barefaced lies

Golfers have to become accustomed to the misfortune of having good shots finish with the ball lying on bare patches of fairway, on paths, or in old divot marks. One of golf's older adages is 'it was never meant to be a fair game anyway'.

Fig. 80 Let the hands lead the clubhead for a low, running shot. Use a three-quarter swing with a stronger club than normal. Restrict the follow-through for a low or punched shot.

The object is to stay calm, not to become tense, and to know how to deal with the situation. The answer is to take a straighter-faced club than you normally would for the distance, settle for a *three-quarter* swing, and *punch* the shot from the *back* of the stance. There will be a real danger of the clubface being turned at impact, so *grip firmly*.

Fig. 81 Grip firmly to prevent the clubhead turning, and punch the ball from the back of the stance, to escape from a divot.

Fig. 82

A Normal swing plane.   **B** Flat swing encourages hook.

C Upright out-to-in swing encourages slice.

12
DIAGNOSING COMMON FAULTS

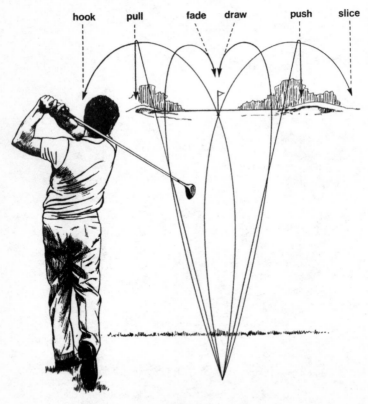

Fig. 83

The golfer has yet to be born who does not occasionally send the ball soaring away with the destructive left-to-right flight of an unwanted slice. What causes this most common and costly of all faults, and what is the cure? If only it were as simple as that. A slice can result from any one of a dozen set-up and swing malfunctions. Consequently, there are just as many possible solutions. Often, to complicate matters even further, a combination of two or more causes has to be untangled. And the same applies to all other faults that you must expect to encounter during your development as a golfer. A primary checklist, that can be useful on the practice ground for the purpose of self-analysis, is given below. However, if the problem persists, then you should seek the help of a professional teacher before it becomes ingrained in the swing as a habit.

The slice

Effect: a 'pure slice' starts the ball left of the target, then the side spin imparted by an open clubface and outside-to-in swing path causes it to curve to the right.

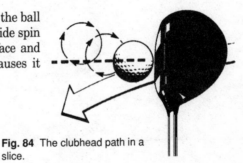

Fig. 84 The clubhead path in a slice.

Causes

A Weak grip, the hands turned too far left, causing only one knuckle of the left hand to show.

B Addressing the ball with an open clubface, or pronating the wrists to open it during the takeaway.

C Faulty set-up with the ball positioned too far forward, causing the hips and shoulders to aim left of the target so that the club will go outside the target line on the backswing.

D Failure to complete the pivot; and starting the downswing with the shoulders instead of a lateral hip movement, i.e. failing to use the legs during the swing.

Fig. 85 The slice.

The hook

Effect: side-spin caused by a closed clubface and inside-to-out swing path giving the right-to-left flight of a hooked shot.

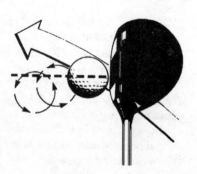

Fig. 86 The clubhead path in a hook.

Causes

A Strong grip with the hands too much to the right, four knuckles of the left hand showing.

B Addressing the ball with a closed clubface, or hooding it on the takeaway.

C Faulty set-up with ball too far back, causing hips and shoulders to aim to the right of the target, creating an excessive in-to-out swing.

D Failure to turn hips and transfer weight to the left side for impact.

Fig. 87 The hook.

The pull

Effect: The ball flies on a straight line left of the target.

Causes

A   The set-up wrongly aimed to the left, with the ball too far forward at the address position.
B   Holding the clubface square to an outside-to-in-swing path.
C   Poor balance, falling back on the right foot during the downswing.

The push

Effect: the ball is hit straight but to the right of the target.

Causes

A   Set-up aimed to the right.
B   Ball too far back in the stance.
C   Going outside the line on the backswing, then looping on the way down to compensate.
D   Failing to clear the hips at impact.

The shank

Effect: the *shank* or *socket* occurs when the ball is struck with the *hosel* rather than the clubface, causing it to fly right at 45°.

Causes

A   Standing too close to the ball and swaying forward on to the toes during the downswing.
B   Flat swing, and rolling the clubface open.
C   Lazy hand action.

Fig. 88 The shank.

The top

Effect: When the ball is *topped* it means that it has been hit high on its perimeter, instead of solidly in the back, causing the ball to travel little or no distance, low to the ground.

Causes

A Angle of attack on ball too steep.
B Too much body action on down-swing.
C Swinging too quickly.
D Standing too close to the ball at address.

Fig. 89 The topped shot: the bottom half of the clubface strikes the top half of the ball.

Skying

Effect: the opposite of topping (although the causes are similar): the ball soars up into the air and consequently loses considerable distance.

Causes

A Poor set-up, encouraging bending of the wrists and lifting of the clubhead too early in the backswing.
B Failure to transfer the weight back to the left foot on the down-swing.
C Angle of attack on the ball is too steep, leading to a chopping action which results in contact being made with the top of the clubhead instead of the middle of the clubface.
D Tilting the shoulders instead of turning on a flat plane.

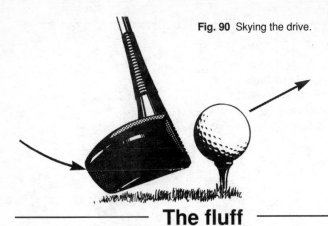

Fig. 90 Skying the drive.

The fluff

Effect: More often known as 'hitting fat' (or hitting thick'), this shot results from the clubhead making contact with the ground before the ball. This will usually turn the clubface away from the square, and the ball can fly in any direction.

Causes

A Angle of attack too flat.
B Hitting too early.
C Not turning the hips out of the way on the downswing.
D Bad posture at address.

Inconsistency

Effect: The worst fault of all, for it means a succession of different mistakes, causing extreme frustration.

Causes

A Bad posture, leading to a poor sense of balance.
B Swinging too quickly.
C Failing to take time to develop a mental picture of what is needed to make the shot a success.

SANDY LYLE **never too young to start**

IAN WOOSNAM from farm to fortune

COLIN MONTGOMERIE consistency rewards well

NICK PRICE a firm and rewarding grip

LAURA DAVIES new image for women's golf

TIGER WOODS master of a classical swing

Costantino Rocca the orthodox Italian

TOM LEHMAN the resolute American

13

THE EVOLUTION OF GOLF AND ITS RULES

Nobody knows where or when golf was invented. In all probability it was not invented at all but just happened as the result of an evolutionary process which began when primitive man developed an instinct, when out hunting with a club in hand, to strike at any inviting object in his path.

Genetic inheritance would certainly explain the spontaneous outbreak of cross country club-and-ball games of uncanny similarity around the world at different periods, including the earliest recorded example, a 'golfing' pharaoh, Japanese Dakyu ('hit ball') of the Nara Period in the first millenium, probably derived from the Chinese game of Suigan, the Roman game of cambuca paganica, and numerous related pastimes in Western Europe.

Exactly when primitive urges among the Scots first expressed them-selves in golf is unknown but the game was banned by royal decree in 1457 so by that time it must have been a well-established and popular sport.

No written or pictorial evidence has been found to tell us what that early golf was like but certain deductions can be made. Since the game was banned, along with football, because men were neglecting their archery practice in readiness for military duties, the implements for golf must have been within the scope of a working man's financial resources, possibly one home-made club and balls of cheap, turned hardwood. The playing area can only have been common ground and the golfers must therefore have shared it with footballers, archers, walkers, rabbit hunters, children at play and housewives hanging their washing to dry on the whins. So golf must have been very infor-mal and the 'course' for the day must have been a case of making it up as you went along.

By the middle of the eighteenth century permanent courses had been established along with rudimentary conventions to regulate play. Courses ranged from four holes to 24. Each had its own rules which were passed down by word of mouth. So, when 'several Gentlemen of Honour skilful in the ancient and healthful exercise of golf' had the idea for an open competition and petitioned the City of Edinburgh for a silver cup for annual competition on their links at Leith, it became necessary to issue a written code of rules and to form a club to admin-ister them. Thus golf began to take a formal shape.

Those original 13 rules were assembled from 340 words, considerably fewer than today's Rules of Golf committees require to compose an explanatory appendix defining the permissable markings on the face of iron clubs.

1 You must tee your ball within a club-length of the hole.
2 Your tee must be upon the ground.
3 You are not to change the ball which you strike off the tee.
4 You are not to remove stones, bones, or any break-club for the sake of playing your ball, except upon the fair green, and that only within a club-length of your ball.
5 If your ball come among water or any watery filth, you are at liberty to take out your ball and throw it behind the hazard six yards at least; you may play it with any club, and allow your adversary a stroke for so getting out your ball.
6 If your balls be found anywhere touching one another, you are to lift the first ball until you play the last.
7 At holing you are to play your ball honestly for the hole, and not to play upon your adversary's ball, not lying in your way to the hole.
8 If you should lose your ball by its being taken up by any other way, you are to go back to the spot where you struck last and drop another ball and allow your adversary a stroke for the misfortune.
9 No man at holding his ball is to be allowed to mark his way to the holes with his club or anything else.
10 If a ball is stop'd by any person, horse, dog, or anything else, the ball so stop'd must be played where it lyes.
11 If you draw your club in order to strike and proceed so far with your stroke as to be bringing down your club, if then your club should break in any way, it is to be accounted a stroke.
12 He whose ball lyes furthest from the hole is obliged to play first.
13 Neither trench, ditch or dyke made for the preservation of the links, nor the Scholar's Holes, nor the Soldiers Lines, shall be accounted a hazard, but the ball is to be taken out, teed, and played with any iron club.

Ten years later when 22 Noblemen and Gentlemen of St Andrews organised their first open competition they adopted the Edinburgh code almost verbatim. At other golfing greens they continued to make their own rules so there was some variation in such details as the distance from the previous hole the ball must be teed.

There was also considerable divergence in the conventions for taking relief. Compare Edinburgh's Rule 5 with the procedure at Bruntsfield Links: 'If your Ball lies among Human Ordure, Cow Dung, or any such nuisance on the fair green, you may upon losing one (stroke), lift it, throw it over your head, behind the nuisance, and play it with any club you please.'

The formation of formal golf clubs was a significant development in the evolution of the rules. In particular, the St Andrews Golf Club, later to become the Royal and Ancient Golf Club of St Andrews, set the pace.

As St Andrews became established as the premier golf club, so other clubs began to follow its lead. For example, and most importantly, when St Andrews revised its course from 22 holes to 18, the 18 holes became the accepted standard for a round of golf.

The custom of teeing your ball alongside the hole into which you had just putted, at increasing distances over the years, began to disappear about 1829, by which time the distance was 20 yards. This was the beginning of the green, or the fair green, as an entity separate from the fairway. That was the genesis of putting, the game within a game, as we know it today.

The introduction in 1848 of the gutta percha ball, at a fraction of the price of the feathery ball, gave a huge stimulus to the growth of the game and the increase in the number of players meant that course maintenance took on a greater importance.

In 1885 Royal Wimbledon petitioned the Royal and Ancient (R and A) club to form an association of clubs and to accept one uniform set of rules. In 1882 the R and A formally accepted responsibility as the ruling body of golf and appointed a Rules of Golf committee.

One of the committee's first actions was to define the teeing ground so the playing area for golf was now established: teeing ground, fairway, and green for each of 18 holes.

Important milestones in the refinement of the game were:

- 1893 Hole codified at 4¹/₄ inches
- 1908 First definitions of the form and make of clubs
- 1920 Lost ball, out of bounds and unplayable ball all subject to stroke and distance procedure
- 1921 First size and weight restrictions imposed on the golf ball
- 1924 Use of steel shafts approved by United States Golf Associations (USGA). (The R and A followed suit in 1929.)
- 1938 The USGA imposed 14 club limit. (The R and A followed in 1939.)

The USGA was formed in 1895 and it assumed the responsibility for making and administering its rules in America and Mexico. Over the years considerable divergences appeared between the American and the R and A codes, most notably in the use of balls of different sizes. In 1951 a conference of the two Rules of Golf committees was called to thrash out a unified code for all the world. With the exception of the ball size and small anomalies in the regulations for amateur status to accommodate social differences, the unification process was completed. Since that time the two Rules of Golf committees have worked in unison.

Complete unity in the playing rules was accomplished in 1988 when the American ball of 1.68-inch minimum diameter and 1.62-ounce maximum weight became the standard ball for all the world.

14

COMMON SENSE AND GOOD MANNERS FORM ETIQUETTE OF THE GAME

The Code of Etiquette for golf is older even than the written laws which govern the game. It is fair to surmise that the earliest of players must at times have requested of their partners or opponents, 'Please don't stand too close when I am swinging', or, perhaps, 'No talking when I am hitting my shot'. All such essential courtesies to encourage enjoyment for everyone on the course, bolstered by the need for guidelines on safety, have now been combined by the government of the game, the Royal and Ancient Golf Club of St Andrews, to form 'Section 1 – Etiquette' as the introduction to the official Rules of Golf.

Over 100 years ago, Horace Hutchinson in the Badminton Library contribution to golf, described the 'Etiquette and behaviour' required for the game in words that few would argue with today. He wrote: 'In connection with the game of golf there are certain points of etiquette which, though not of such a nature as to fall within the jurisdiction of the written law, are pretty accurately defined by the sanction of custom.

'Breach of these observances is not punished by the loss of the hole or of a stroke, but rather by the loss of social status in the golfing world. You do not exact an immediate penalty from him who thus outrages "les convenances"; but in your heart of hearts you propose to yourself the severest of all forms of punishment, viz. never to play with him again.'

The Code of Etiquette as now defined by the R and A through its Rules of Golf Committee, and in an extremely useful, illustrated booklet made available to all by the English Golf Union, gives clear guidance on the aspects of safety; consideration for others; the speed at which games should be played; priorities to be respected and care of the course.

Common sense dictates safety: don't stand near to a player hitting a shot, and don't take a practice swing without first ensuring that it is safe to do so. And never hit until the players ahead are well out of range. Though regrettable, it is possible that in certain circumstances – an unseen player, for example, suddenly emerging after being hidden in trees – a misjudgement can create an element of danger, in which case the warning cry of 'Fore' must be made loud and clear.

Likewise, good manners dictate consideration for other players. Concentration is absolutely vital for playing good and consistent golf. Acts of distraction, such as talking or moving while an opponent or partner plays, are totally unacceptable. At best it is thoughtlessness; at worst gamesmanship, and this can never be tolerated in golf.

Pace of play is one of golf's most serious and enduring problems. The enjoyment of the game is lost when those ahead play so slowly that your match and others behind are kept waiting on every shot. The delay inevitably accumulates until 'traffic jams' are created, and the tees at short holes especially can become congested with groups waiting in a queue. There can be no enjoyment in playing golf this way.

It is essential to play without delay. If a ball is lost and proves difficult to find don't use the 'five-minute rule' limit for searching as an excuse to keep the match behind waiting. Wave them through and allow play to keep flowing. On completing a hole quit the green immediately. There is nothing more infuriating than watching the group ahead putt out, then standing still to laboriously compare scores and mark scorecards before moving to the next tee. When a match plays so slowly that it loses a complete hole on those in front, then it should observe the etiquette of the game by calling through those immediately waiting behind.

An enjoyable pace of game also requires four-ball and three-ball matches to invite two-ball matches to play through. But a player on his own has no standing, of course. He is not entitled to expect any form of preferential treatment. But what is an enjoyable and acceptable pace of play? It is possible to play too quickly as opposed to the far more frequent sin of too slowly. It is aggravating for the orderly process of play on a busy course to be disturbed by a match intent on hurrying. Golf is not meant to be a leisurely crawl for the tortoise, and neither is it meant to be a race for the hare. There is, and it has to be respected at all times, a happy medium.

Some clubs go so far as to publish on their notice boards recommended times for the completion of 18 holes for singles, three-ball and four-ball games. These naturally vary from club to club in recognising the severity of their courses. Obviously, for example, it will need more time at Wentworth to play the championship West Course with its tight tree-lined fairways than the shorter and more forgiving East Course. Ideally, however, an average of 2 hours and 40 minutes for singles, 3 hours and 15 minutes for three-balls and 3 hours and 40 minutes for four-balls are sensible targets.

The golfer's duty to 'take care of the course' has a clear guide – he should leave the course in the condition he expects to find it. This means replacing divots, repairing pitchmarks on every green, and carefully raking a bunker after playing a recovery shot. There are few greater and more unfair tests of patience and temperament than entering a bunker to find the ball buried in a footprint left by a previous player. It is an unthinking and downright unsocial offence. Indeed, in professional tournament golf it is a punishable offence. An offending player is fined, and rightly so.

As the game of golf continues to gain popularity, become more crowded, and move with the times, not always for the good it has to be admitted, the Code of Etiquette expands in many unwritten ways. While the mobile telephone may be a great convenience in everyday life for some,

it can be infuriating to others on the course. Good, traditional clubs such as Sunningdale forbid the use of mobile telephones in the club-house and on the course. If you must, the committee rules, find a quiet corner in the car park. In Continental Europe it is frequently necessary to prove ownership of a golfer's insurance before playing. While this attitude is less prevalent in Britain it is no less wise and necessary to have an insurance to cover not only the loss of equipment but also per-sonal liability for costly damages when accidents occur.

Remember – common sense and good manners will always be the best guide to playing the game in a way that permits safety and enjoyment for all.

15

LOOK AND LEARN

The challenge of *Teach Yourself Golf* invites several solutions. A balanced combination of them all will achieve the best results for the beginner and advanced player alike.

Instructional books and articles can provide a solid foundation if sensibly used. There is no purpose to be served in studying the relatively short and fast swing techniques of Corey Pavin for moving the ball either way on a controlled flight if you have still to master the basic need to consistently hit the ball reasonably straight. Far better then to watch the balance, rhythm and timing achieved by the likes of Ernie Els and Nick Faldo, go away and imitate on the practice ground.

So much can be learned studying the best players in the game. Not that they ever claim perfection. Faldo, for example, and he has accumulated a whole collection of major championship titles, never ceases to learn more about the golf swing. The best place to watch and learn from the stars of the game is on the practice ground at a tournament. It is an opportunity that young, up-and-coming professionals are themselves quick to take. When the game's most successful golfer of all time, Jack Nicklaus, begins his practice routine at an Open Championship they will often quit their own preparations to watch and hopefully learn the ingredients of greatness.

For the beginner the orthodox swing of Italy's Costantino Rocca has a lot to offer; those who lack height should study how Ian Woosman still manages to generate more hitting power than most of his much bigger fellow professionals. It's called timing, and that is something the most advanced player can learn more about by watching the former Masters champion.

When it is not possible to visit a tournament to learn there are many instructional videos by top professionals advising on how they play, and how you might, too, with enough dedication and determination. In choosing your video mentor, however, it is generally wise to become the disciple of a teacher with a similar physique to your own. Obviously a 6ft 3in beginner will have problems trying to imitate the swing of 5ft 4in Woosnam. Better to settle for a Faldo video.

And do not overlook the fact that Faldo, Woosnam and a lot of their world-class colleagues are anxious learners too. Quite often they can be seen with their coaches or 'gurus' on the practice ground at a tournament. They may be winning £1 million in a single season but they still take lessons, and that is something the beginner and advanced player needs to understand. There is no substitute for the occasional, fine-tuning lesson from a good professional teacher to ensure, among other things, that your practice sessions are not resulting in the creation and grooving of a fault. It is the best money to be spent in golf, for the way to enjoy the game to the full is to play well. There is not a lot of joy in continually having to look for your golf ball wide of the fairway.

It is well worth watching the following outstanding players on the practice ground at a tournament and then trying to imitate their strong points.

Fearless and natural
Severiano Ballesteros

Born Padrena, Spain, 9 April 1957

Many have contributed to European golf's rise to world-class recognition in all areas, but nobody has made it more exciting than Severiano Ballesteros with his cavalier and fearless use of a marvellously natural talent. He has been responsible for widening the appeal of the game in Europe in much the same way as Arnold Palmer inspired the modern golf boom in America with his swashbuckling approach.

Seve's uncle, Ramon Sota, and three older brothers, Baldomero, Manuel and Vicente, are all golf professionals, and it was with their encouragement that he first began developing the aggressive style of play that made him a multiple winner of major championships and, at his peak, the best golfer in the world.

As a youngster he used a cut-down three iron to hit shots on the Pedrena beach when not earning pocket money as a caddie. Only 16 when he turned professional, Ballesteros was the Open champion and a Ryder Cup international at 22, and the youngest-ever winner of the Masters at Augusta at 23. More than 70 tournament titles worldwide have fallen to him along with almost £5 million prize money. Rightly, Seve's tremendous contribution to golf was recognised with his being selected to captain Europe's 1997 Ryder Cup team at Valderrama, Spain.

The most exciting sight in golf has long been Seve Ballesteros on a charge, driving prodigious distances, scorning danger, and, as he so often has to do, escaping from trouble in amazing fashion. There has never been a better scrambler, and a fine touch is equally as evident as his exceptional power. Seve has always had a marvellous 'never say die' attitude, and although he eventually tried to become technically more correct, his real strength was his aggressiveness and ability to think and play his way out of seemingly desperate situations. It is one thing in golf to score well when you are playing well, but you still have to get round the course when you are below form. Then, more than ever, you have to think your way round, play to the strengths you do have on that particular day, be positive, don't allow yourself to become despondent – be like Seve, never give up. Study the patient manner in which he so often turns a crisis into a birdie opportunity.

Determination and dedication
Nick Faldo

Born Welwyn Garden City, 18 July 1957

Determination and dedication are two vital pillars on which all successful golfers build their careers, and there is no more inspiring example to study than Nick Faldo who never ceases to seek higher standards for his exceptional talent. Indeed, on reaching the peak of the European tournament scene in 1983 with five wins in a single season, he sacrificed the next two years to totally rebuild his already enviable golf swing in a search for greater consistency under pressure at world-class level. It was an act greeted with general amazement at the time, but his collection of major championship titles and Ryder Cup heroics since has proved the wisdom of his bold decision.

Swimming and cycling dominated Faldo's interests in sport as a schoolboy until, at 14, he watched Jack Nicklaus on television, playing in the Masters at Augusta. He immediately became a golf addict with the belief it was a game he could play well. After winning the English Amateur Championship he turned professional at 19, and more than 30 top tournament victories and £5 million prize money winnings later he remains as determined and dedicated as ever to his ambitions.

Long hours on the practice ground, many with his coach David Leadbetter, have given him the exceptional consistency he knew would be needed to make him a great champion. Memorable moments of proof include his first Open Championship win at Muirfield in 1987 when he defied the extreme pressures of the final round by scoring par at all 18 holes.

Watching Nick Faldo play golf is a marvellously instructive lesson. All the essential fundaments are to be seen in his swing, beginning with the way he sets himself solidly over the ball, knees slightly bent at the address, and correct grip. On the backswing his upper body turns, the left arm rotates in sympathy with this turn so that at the top the clubface is in a square or slightly open position and the shaft of the club points at the target. The resistance of the lower part of the body this far gives him a beautiful, tight, coil effect. Then the hips and knees become the leaders of the downswing with the club rotating back on an inside-to-in arc, square at impact, as he swings well within himself to maintain a fine balance throughout. Nick's great strength is that he is always able to have the same tempo because he doesn't try to be the world's longest hitter – he gives priority to rhythm and balance.

Success beyond compare
Jack Nicklaus

Born Columbus, Ohio, 21 January 1940

Still building on more than 100 tournament wins, including 18 major professional championships for a record that has no serious challenger in sight, Jack Nicklaus is unquestionably the most successful golfer ever. As a junior and college golfer he first displayed the exceptional power and strategical ability to outthink a course and his challengers that eventually raised him to the status of legend.

Nicklaus began collecting important titles by twice winning the United States Amateur, and gave notice of what more was to come when in 1960, while still an amateur, he finished second to Arnold Palmer in the US Open. Two years later, for his first success as a rookie professional, he won the championship with Palmer as the runner-up.

By the age of 25 he had joined the most elite club in world golf by winning all four major championships. Now his total collection has grown to read: 6 Masters; 5 US PGAs; 4 US Opens; 3 British Opens. Arguably, his finest moment was in 1986 when he played the final 10 holes of the Augusta National Course in seven under par to become the oldest winner of the Masters.

Nicklaus has contributed in countless ways to the well-being of golf throughout the world, and both the British Open and Ryder Cup owe much to his active support. While still a successful Senior, he now largely concentrates on business interests, especially as a prolific designer of courses in many countries.

Great mind, great attitude, great concentration – Jack Nicklaus has it all, and that's why he is probably the best golfer who ever lived. His natural instinct is to play left to right, and he doesn't fight it. This is an important lesson for all amateurs to learn: don't try to go against natural instinct. If your natural shot is right to left then accept it and develop a controlled draw. But, if like Nicklaus you are a natural left-to-right hitter of the ball, learn to control a fade. It is so important to have a natural shot that will stand up under pressure. Nicklaus's whole pre-shot routine and demeanour should be studied by every golfer who wants to improve. He will waggle, address the ball, waggle again, re-address and keep doing so until he is comfortable, totally concentrated and confident. Note especially the intense concentration that is so much of his putting method. It helps explain why he has been a winner for almost 40 years.

Seeing is believing
John Daly

Born Carmichael, California, 28 April 1966

The biggest galleries in golf are drawn to John Daly whose uninhibited use of enormous power has to be seen to be believed. While contradicting the textbook in many ways, however, he also possesses a fine touch and in between tempestuous moments his wealth of talent swept him to the rare feat of two major championship victories before the age of 30.

John's ability to consistently drive the ball beyond 300 yards was honed on the satellite tour in America and during visits to South Africa where he won two titles without attracting attention, or suspicion that he was a future superstar. All that changed in 1991 when, as a rookie on the US Tour, he received an eleventh-hour call as ninth reserve to complete the field for the PGA Championship. He drove through the night to be at Crooked Stick, Indiana, in time, and went on to decisively beat the world's best golfers for the title.

Daly's philosophy of 'grip it and rip it' was condemned by traditionalists as totally unsuited to the Old Course at St Andrews when he came to challenge for the 1995 Open Championship. Again he surprised them all with a marvellously balanced display of power and delicate golf to win. He has been likened to a hurricane for his golf –

dangerous, wild, unpredictable, exciting to watch. All of which will continue to make him a gallery favourite wherever he plays.

When watching John Daly drive a golf ball it is too easy to become mesmerised by the distance he achieves and his flouting of textbook principles to complete the backswing with the clubhead so far below the horizontal that it finishes down by the left hip. It is an extraordinary style, all his own, which generates such power at impact that exceptional flexibility and healthy back muscles are vital to avoid injury. Inevitably, when the clubface fails to be square to the target at impact a search for the ball well wide of the fairway results. When found, he then demonstrates with his recovery shots a superbly fine touch for such a powerfully strong man. In studying his unique style, however, look at his exemplary address position, and envy the suppleness that allows him to complete a perfect shoulder turn.

—— Flying to the top of the world ——
Greg Norman

Born Queensland, Australia, 2 February 1955

The Australian, who for so long reigned over the golf rankings as the world No. 1, took up the game at the comparatively late age of 16. He made up for lost time in an enormous hurry, however, and was playing to a handicap of scratch after only two years. When he turned professional in 1976, a tough decision because he had earlier set his mind on training to be a pilot, his career continued at an equally hectic pace. A winner after just four tournaments, named for World Cup international duty after only six, he has since amassed more than 70 victories in 13 counties and over £8 million in official prize money, amply enough to afford his own private jet aircraft.

One of the most gifted players in the history of the game, but in some respects among the most cruelly treated by fate, Norman won his first major championship at the 1986 Open at Turnberry and took the title again at Royal St George's, Sandwich, in 1993 with a record score. At other times, however, his major championship ambitions suffered painful misfortunes. The 1986 US PGA crown was denied him when Bob Tway holed a bunker shot on the final hole, and Larry Mize chipped in to defeat him in a play-off for the 1988 Masters. Norman has lost play-offs for all four major championships, but the most bitter experience of his life was losing the 1996 Masters to Nick Faldo.

However, his successes far outweigh his disappointments, and a powerful, confident style of play and generous personality make him a crowd favourite throughout the world of golf.

Over the years Greg Norman has been regarded as the most consistent, straightest and longest hitter off the tee. He drives so well because he is one of the few players at the top of the game who stands very close to the ball and this enables him to adopt an upright stance. It means he can produce a terrific turn on the backswing and then clear his body so rapidly in the downswing that exceptional clubhead speed is achieved. Note the wide, one-piece takeaway, and how his head remains steady throughout the swing – essential for the consistent accuracy needed to be a major champion.

The burden of fame
Ernie Els

Born Johannesburgh, 17 October 1969

Exceptional potential at one sport always has its problems for a youngster. South Africa's Ernie Els, at the age of 14, was excelling and attracting 'star of the future' attention in tennis (he was already the Eastern Transvaal's senior champion), cricket and rugby. Fortunately, he turned to golf and began justifying his decision at a breathtaking pace. At 15, and with a handicap of scratch, he became the World Junior champion. One year later and he was the youngest-ever holder of the South African Amateur title. His entry into the professional ranks was even more exciting and he swiftly established himself as a world-class prospect by winning South Africa's Open, PGA and Masters championships all in the 1992 season before moving on to Europe and the United States.

Astonishingly, as a rookie on the US Tour in 1994, he won the US Open Championship, and along with it that same season the Desert Classic in Dubai, the Sarazen World Open in America, the Johnnie Walker World Championship in Jamaica, and, at Wentworth, the

World Match-Play Championship which he successfully defended the following two years. Just how far the potential he showed as a youngster will finally reach is one of golf's most fascinating imponderables.

Ernie Els has an excellent technique allied to an exceptional rhythm. No matter how much pressure he is under, Ernie is able to maintain his rhythm, width through the ball and perfect balance. If he doesn't stay at the top of the game for the next decade or more, it won't be for lack of powerful encouragement. Jack Nicklaus and Gary Player are only two of many who believe that his still-maturing talent can take command of the game. He defies what could be the handicap of a heavyweight build – 6ft 3in and 15 stone – with a beautiful, full, languid swing. Ernie resolutely avoids becoming too deeply involved in the mechanics of the golf swing, and watching him is an abject lesson in the value of 'keeping it simple'. But the most instructive guidance of all comes when he faces the need to hit a really long ball. He will then slow his swing even more, and rely on rhythm and timing.

Champion pioneer
Bernhard Langer

Born Anhausen, Germany, 27 August 1957

The route of boy caddie to distinguished professional has been followed by many, but few with more successful determination than Bernhard Langer, the first German to win a major championship and to attain Ryder Cup status.

As a seven-year-old growing up in Bavaria where his father had settled after escaping from a Russian prisoner-of-war train destined for Siberia, Bernhard began contributing to the family income by working as a junior caddie outside of school hours. His passion for the game, and a natural talent, led to him turning professional at 15, then leaping to international recognition in 1979 with an astounding 17-shot victory at the World Under-25s Championship. The following year Langer began establishing another record on the European Tour, his consistency leading to at least one win for 17 consecutive seasons, and a run of 68 tournaments without missing a half-way qualifying cut.

Golf was very much a minor sport in Germany until Langer became a national hero in 1985 by beating the best players in the world to win the coveted US Masters title. He repeated the feat eight years later and established himself as an exceptional international champion by accumulating more than 40 victories in 16 countries. He now applies the same painstaking diligence to his growing business interests, including golf course design.

Watching Bernhard Langer and other great players shows that there is no set method of putting. Everyone has to experiment and devise a personal approach to this 'game within a game' while obviously observing certain principles: head steady over the ball to allow proper lining up of the putter; club low back and through the ball. Bernhard has done this to overcome his confrontations with the putting 'yips', the most painful and costly of all golf's afflictions. Remarkably, he has fought the problem that has ruined others' careers so successfully that he became recognised at various times as the best putter on both the European and US Tours. His first answer was to adopt a unique split-handed putting style which entailed clamping the grip of the putter to the inside of the left arm, so keeping both wrists firm. Since then he has resorted to the long putter for more consistent success. In deciding a putting method be like Bernhard – experiment to decide which style works best for you; be flexible and ready to adapt.

Calm and cool winner
Fred Couples

Born Seattle, 3 October 1959

Born into a seriously sports-minded family – his father played baseball as a part-time professional and golf for enjoyment – Fred Couples would most likely have excelled at any of the games he tried as a youngster. Happily, his father, who worked in the Seattle Parks and Recreation Department, encouraged the choice of golf, and wise, rewarding advice it has proved.

Fred has developed two of the most enviable assets in all golf – a seemingly effortless swing of exceptional power, and a temperament that makes him a calm and cool winner under the severest pressure.

As a junior, he made a shrewd business deal that was to lay the foundations for a career that has been worth over £6 million in prize money. He offered his part-time help to a local golf club in return for free use of the driving range. Once accepted, he took every opportunity to practise.

The result was fast and furious progress in strict contrast to his slow, lazy swing and ultra laid-back approach to the game. By 18 he was the Washington State Open champion, and during his three years at Houston University on a golf scholarship he was twice named All-American. On the US Tour he became known as 'Boom, Boom' because of the power that has guided him to multiple tournament successes, including the Masters major championship, in the United States, Caribbean, Europe, Middle East and Far East. Among his most notable achievements was teaming with Davis Love III to win the World Cup four years in succession for the United States.

Fred Couples has a great swing and he is one of the longest hitters in the world. His action, involving relatively little use of the legs, looks so effortless and simple, but the truth, as many have discovered, is that it is desperately difficult to copy. He has an unusually full turn on the backswing which he completes with a pronounced pause before starting down, and his right arm tends to fly a little at the top which gives him even more of a turn. He is very flat footed on the downswing so that all of his power is coming from the waist up. Extremely effective, but a style far from easy for the average golfer to adopt.

Never too young to start
Sandy Lyle

Born Shrewsbury, 2 February 1958

The first evidence of Sandy Lyle being a golfer on the way to winning both the Open Championship and the US Masters is a photograph of him at the age of three, pulling his set of miniature clubs on a specially made trolley. He was then capable of hitting a ball 50 yards, and power became the cornerstone of his successful career, both as an amateur and a professional.

After playing for England at boy, youth and full international level,

Sandy eventually opted for the Scottish nationality of his father, Alex, then the professional at Hawkestone Park, and a teacher of international repute. Sandy was so well tutored that he held a scratch handicap as a teenager, was a junior champion at 14, the youngest-ever winner of the English Amateur Open at 17, and a Walker Cup player at 19.

When he turned professional in 1977 he announced his intentions in the clearest of terms by winning the Qualifying School tournament for admission to PGA European Tour membership. Between 1979 and 1985 he headed the Order of Merit three times, never being below fifth in the rankings. The peak of his career undoubtedly came in 1985 when he won the Open championship at Royal St George's, Sandwich. Sandy, a Ryder Cup stalwart, immediately dedicated himself to claiming another major championship, and this he did in 1988 by becoming the first British player to win the US Masters. His final-hole fairway bunker shot with a 7 iron has become part of golf lore.

While enjoying the heights of success and the pains of struggling through unrewarding phases of his career, Sandy has won friends with his self-deprecating charm. He also revealed a quick wit when, on winning the US Tournament Players Championship, he was asked what the difference was between that event and the Open Championship. 'About 150 years,' he immediately responded, to the approval of all British golfers.

Sandy himself wouldn't describe his swing as a thing of beauty, but all the basic fundamentals are there for the observer to note and digest. He personally describes the essentials as 'a comfortable set-up, a good extension, start down with the legs, think tempo, and give it a good old whack.' The result for Sandy has been a remarkable 123 miles-an-hour measurement of his clubhead speed at impact.

From farm to fortune
Ian Woosnam

Born Oswestry, 2 March 1958

Self-belief is essential at every level of golf, from the immediate shot to be hit to ambitions for the distant future. Three visits to the annual PGA European Tour Qualifying School tested Ian Woosnam's resolve to the cruellest limits, but he never doubted his ability to be a champion. He proved himself right by winning the US Masters and becoming world No 1.

Life has been all about creating and mastering challenges for Ian, a Welshman whose 5ft 4in build has much to do with his pugnacious character. Rather than accept being labelled as one of the smallest players in professional golf, he set about gaining respect as one of the most powerful and longest hitters in the game. He developed his strength working on his father's farm as a boy, and his exceptionally powerful hands and arms owe much to the long days he spent wrestling with the driving wheel of a tractor bouncing over ploughed fields. Football and boxing marked him out as a fearless competitor at an early age, but it was golf that interested him most. He played for Shropshire as an amateur and became all the more determined when a team-mate, Sandy Lyle, captured more attention.

Woosnam, who now has his own jet aircraft, shared a battered van when he first joined the European Tour, hoping that times would get better. He knew for sure that they would when he followed in the footsteps of Bernhard Langer and won the World Under-25 Championship to capture international recognition. In 1987 the improvement he enjoyed stretched to his becoming the first European Tour player to win £1 million worldwide in a single year. Now he is approaching £5 million in total career winnings.

The fluent swing of Ian Woosnam is packed with power. His strong arms, great timing and perfect balance combine to show that the ability to hit a golf ball a long way doesn't demand a huge physique. Indeed, his technique is envied by many of the world's best players for he swings the club just about as well as it can be. He stands upright to the ball, using what height he has to the full, and that way he achieves a great turn of the body. Ian displays all the important aspects of the golf swing: good posture, correct grip, strong arm rotation on the backswing to open up the club. He generates terrific clubhead speed with more use of arms than legs, swings a little inside to out, more than most others, but being quite small he does need the help of a controlled hook or draw.

Consistency rewards well
Colin Montgomerie

Born Glasgow, 23 June 1963

The transition from successful amateur to tournament professional becomes more difficult each year as ever-increasing prize money for greater incentive inevitably raises the standards demanded of those who play the game for a living. Indeed, there have been several winners of the British and United States Amateur Championships who have taken on the challenge but failed to last the pace.

Colin Montgomerie, however, is a notable exception and the speed of his leap from the amateur ranks to the very peak of world golf is an inspiring example of what can be achieved with the right talent and unrelenting determination. Steeped in the game all his life as the Scottish son of a golf club secretary, Montgomerie was runner-up for the 1984 British Amateur title – beaten by Jose Maria Olazabal, the young Spaniard who was to go on and win the US Masters – before capturing both the Scottish stroke-play and match-play Amateur Championships.

He used a golf scholarship at Houston Baptist University in Texas to groove a superb swing while also spending enough time in the classroom to receive a degree in business management and law. After two Walker Cup appearances he turned professional in 1987 and began demonstrating his winning and remarkably consistent ways two years later by becoming the Portuguese Open champion with 11 shots to spare. While a Ryder Cup regular and persistent No 1 on the European Tour rankings, Montgomerie, among the most articulate of professionals, raced past the £4 million mark in the first nine years of his prize money career. Even then he was convinced that the best was still to come.

Along with a good golfing brain, Colin Montgomerie has an excellent repeating golf swing. He plays a left-to-right shot; he doesn't cut the ball, but fades it with control. He aims a little parallel left of target – he doesn't stand open – and he employs a slightly upright arm swing with quite a flat shoulder turn. This enables him to approach the ball at a shallow angle, throwing the clubface under the ball which keeps it open through the shot, and this is what gives him the fade as opposed to a cut. Monty swings well within himself and his beautifully balanced follow-through and high finish are models to copy.

A firm and rewarding grip
Nick Price

Born Durban, January 28 1957

Born in South Africa, raised in Zimbabwe, a winner in his formative years on the European Tour before moving to the United States, Nick Price is an immensely talented, truly international tournament golfer. He has the proven ability to play in any country, master the varying conditions, and win.

Price started golf at the age of eight, and showed his liking for globe-trotting challenges at 17 when he travelled to San Diego, California, to win the World Junior Championship. Then his inevitable entry into the professional game was delayed for two years while he did National Service in the Rhodesian Air Force. Once into the prize money ranks he began his winning ways in Africa in 1979 and has since won over £6 million and more than 30 important titles in 10 different countries. For a while, however, the success he wanted, the Open Championship, proved the most elusive.

He might have won in 1982 when at Royal Troon he came to the last six holes with a lead of three shots. But the greater experience of Tom Watson prevailed in the end. Then at Royal Lytham in 1988 he held a lead of two shots going into the final round of the Open. A closing score of 69 could well have won him the title, but it didn't for Seve Ballesteros fashioned a brilliant 65 to snatch victory. When Price's perseverance was eventually rewarded with his Open victory at Turnberry in 1994 – the year he also had a repeat US PGA Championship success – he revealed his relief by saying: 'I once had my left hand on the cup; then I had my right hand on the cup; now I have both hands on the cup, and it feels great.'

Nick Price, of course, stands among the best golfers in the world. He puts a good grip and technique to work with powerful hands, and he is one of the very few champions who plays with a strong wrist at the top; there is little wrist cock to be seen in his swing. He and Nick Faldo, who have the same coach, David Leadbetter, show a lot of similarities, like the lovely rotation of the left arm on the backswing to open the club. Price displays all the correct fundamentals, including a big shift to transfer the weight from the left side to the right for the backswing, then on the downswing getting it back to the left side, and a perfectly balanced follow-through despite his swinging a lot harder than Faldo.

New image for women's golf
Laura Davies

Born Coventry, 5 October 1963

Laura Davies, certainly the longest hitter and arguably the most naturally talented player in women's professional golf, shuns the trend of modern champions to have their careers guided by a 'guru' coach. The tremendous and consistent international success she has enjoyed – culminating in her being ranked World No 1 – is owed very largely to various forms of self teaching. Laura has never favoured formal lessons, preferring instead to learn from watching others and then experimenting to adapt what she approved to her own benefit. She is a marvellous example of 'Teach Yourself Golf' at work.

Such is the wealth of her natural talent, however, that she spends less time on the practice ground than most of the challengers she regularly faces, while approaching a total of 50 tournament victories, including the British and United States Open Championships. When Laura was introduced to golf at the age of 14 she began improving a handicap of 36 to plus five by the time she played in the 1984 Curtis Cup seven years later, after having helped fund her golf with part-time work as a supermarket shelf stacker and petrol pump attendant. The following season, as a rookie, she began competing for her now massive collection of professional titles and immediately headed the European Order of Merit.

Laura has used her talent to do a great pioneering job for European golf. When first invited in 1987 to contest a tournament on the highly demanding United States women's tour, the authorities rejected her entry. Her response was to win the US Women's Open later that same year, a feat that then encouraged the US LPGA Tour to amend its constitution in order to offer her automatic membership. It was a wise move – she became a major attraction in America and the rest of the world.

Powerfully built, and 5ft 10in tall, Laura Davies can drive close to 300 yards. Her confidence allows her to attack the ball, and the message Laura has to offer lady golfers in general is that they can hit harder than they think they should. Laura goes after every shot with very impressive freedom of movement, and is another good example of enjoying success because she plays to her strengths. She knows she is a long hitter so she takes the driver as often as she can, and attacks the course in order to make the most of the advantage she has over the rest of the field. Her technique is good, the grip and posture at set-up are right, and she is also to be envied for her delicate short game and ability to manufacture shots that would please Seve Ballesteros any day.

An Extraordinary Talent
Tiger Woods

Born Cypress, California, 30 December 1975

The fear that accompanies youngsters of exceptional promise in any sport is that the demand to sustain progress through all levels will make them victims of the 'burn out' factor. It has afflicted many thousands, especially in golf where the mental pressures increase with every raising of ambition. But in Tiger Woods, whose extraordinary talent was introduced to the golf world at the age of two when he putted against Bob Hope on a TV show, there is unquestionable proof that a prodigy can be successfully guided from cradle to major championship.

Tiger (full name: Eldrick Tiger Woods), named after a Vietnamese soldier befriended by his soldier father during the Vietnam war, scored 48 for nine holes when three, and went on to collect a store of youngest-ever records as a unique winner of three successive United States Junior and Amateur championships.

He thrived on the pressures of public expectation on entering the professional ranks in 1996 at 20, cutting short his Stanford University education to win two of the eight US PGA Tour events he played and was named Rookie of the Year. The 1997 season showed the full extent of his abnormal ability: he became the first to win more than 2,000,000 US dollars, and his four tournament victories included the most remarkable US Masters ever as the youngest winner – by a record 12 shots.

All this success has come from the long and dedicated development of an absolutely classical, firm, three-quarter swing in which every component is a lesson to be copied. Tiger is renowned, of course, for his prodigious distance with all clubs, the result of generating exceptionally fast clubhead speed through the ball.

Tiger is a great example of getting the fundamentals right. He has a wonderful posture, stands tall to the ball with knees nicely flexed, and concentrates on a full body rotation. Obviously, he learned the importance of getting the grip right at a very early age, and this has been the solid foundation on which his incredible ability has flourished. His swing – inside going back, inside track on the downswing and follow through – will certainly stand the test of time.

The orthodox Italian Costantino Rocca

Born Bergamo, 4 December 1956

The enjoyment Costantino Rocca gains and shows with an infectious smile from having reached the front-rank of international golf is strengthened by the memories of all that he had to endure along the way. As a boy expected to help support his hard-working family in Bergamo, Rocca devoted his out-of-school hours to working at the local golf club as a caddie. The sound, orthodox swing that has now made him a respected European Tour winner and the first Italian to play for Europe in the Ryder Cup was learned watching, analysing, and adapting the styles of the best club members who employed him to carry their clubs.

On leaving school his life became even harder. He went to work in a factory making polystyrene boxes, and all of his eight years there he dreamed of escaping to create a successful career in golf. The best he initially managed was to take the job of caddie master at the Bergamo Golf Club. But it was a start. He remained determined enough to turn professional at the relatively late age of 24, and began serving a tournament apprenticeship that tested his resolve to the limit. He went to the annual PGA European Tour Qualifying School four times and eventually resorted to the Challenge Tour, the satellite division, vowing to earn promotion to the main tour the hard way. He succeeded. Then came another four years of gathering experience while never losing faith in his ability to reach the top. The year 1993 proved him right and all the gruelling work he had put into building his career was rewarded with two Tour wins in France. He had become the Happy And Contented Italian, and his smile showed it.

Costantino has a very orthodox swing and that has been the basis of his consistent play through the years wherever he competes in the world. He has a good grip and posture, and a most wonderful, flat shoulder turn with an upright swing of the arms. He shifts his weight perfectly, keeps everything as simple as possible, maintains a good rhythm, and this is the foundation of his success. It is a method well worth trying to copy. There are many lessons to be learned from watching Costantino Rocca play golf, beginning with his 'enjoy the game' approach. Even under the severest pressure he will continue to show his enjoyment of golf.

The resolute American Tom Lehman

Born Austin, Minnesota, 7 March 1959

For as long as golf has been played, 500 years in one form or another, the 'secret' of success has been like the crock of gold waiting to be found. As a single key to unravelling all, it doesn't exist. Many factors combine to encourage the ability to play the game consistently well, but if there is one element of supreme, vital importance on which the development of all others will depend, it is persistence. And it is this that brought Tom Lehman through the learning ranks of golf to win the Open Championship.

Nothing comes easily in golf, and Lehman's progress testifies to this fact. When he attracted serious international attention in 1995 by earning selection for the United States Ryder Cup team, his biographer fairly described him as 'the role model for every struggling player in the wilderness of professional golf – a resolute man who persevered his way into the big time and big money.'

Three punishing years on the US Tour from 1985–89, in which he never finished better than 158th on the money list with total earnings of just £25,000, did nothing for his standard of living but a lot for his determination. Still believing that he had the ability to reach the top, Tom set off to gain experience on international circuits including Asia and South Africa. When he returned to America he used success on the Hogan (satellite) Tour to gain promotion for another attempt at the main US Tour. He never ceased to flourish, not even when diagnosed with cancer of the colon. Six weeks after an operation he won a tournament, and more of his perseverance was seen when, immediately after narrowly losing the 1996 US Open, he travelled to Royal Lytham to make amends by winning the British Open.

The strength of Tom Lehman's game lies in his exceptional rhythm. He is one of the few top-class professionals who plays a little bit 'shut' – he has the clubhead slightly shut at the address, he takes it back shut and he actually swings on an inside-to-out path. All this results in a consistent draw. In some respects he has an old-fashioned swing, for years ago in-to-out was very much favoured. But one of the most important things in golf is to know your own swing, and Tom certainly does. He is aware of his strengths, his rhythm and controlled right-to-left flight path, and he knows his weakness which is why you will very rarely see him attempt to hit the ball left to right for a fade.

16

BRAINS BEFORE BRAWN

The recurring impression gained by the average amateur golfer on watching a top tournament professional in action is that the expert appears to strike the ball with far less power to achieve considerably more distance. Only up to a point is this true. Certainly, the lazy swing of, say, Fred Couples, compares drastically with a great many handicap players whose desperation for distance is answered with an uncontrolled thrashing at the ball from the very start of the downswing. Couples and his fellow champions do apply tremendous power – they frequently record clubhead speeds of around 120 mph – but where it matters: in the hitting zone, 12 inches before and through the ball. They rely on balance and rhythm to guide the clubface back square to the target at impact, and timing dictates the moment full power is applied. Unleashing power at the start of the downswing – hitting from the top – wrecks balance, rhythm and timing to the point that most of the clubhead speed is spent before impact.

This is the most basic of the 'brains before brawn' lessons to be learned from the best professionals, and there are many more. Ask the likes of Nick Faldo the most important measurement in golf and he will most probably say: 'The six inches between the ears.' What he means, of course, is that good golf cannot be played without using the brain. While conscientiously working on the technical aspect of the game, too many amateurs, particularly beginners, pay too little attention to the importance of the mental side of golf.

How often have we heard a tournament winner say how much he has benefited from improving his temperament, staying calm, playing one

shot at a time, and, essentially, adopting sound course management by thinking properly. Certainly, temper is the ruination of any golfer. There have been few hot-blooded champions. The great Ben Hogan, known as the 'Ice Man' because of his indifference to pressure, reacted to a wayward shot with nothing more than a stare. To become upset over a missed putt is to invite similar misfortune with the next. Remaining relaxed and calm is never more important than when in trouble on the course. It may not be easy, but it is as essential in golf as it is in life.

Take as an example Sandy Lyle when he won the US Masters. He was in serious trouble on the final hole after driving into a bunker. But he pushed his disappointment into the background, stayed calm, observed the important principle of 'positive thinking at all times', and as a result hit a marvellous 7-iron recovery to within birdie distance of the flagstick. There is no way he could have done this had he allowed himself to become upset over his drive.

There was another striking example of staying cool, calm and collected when Europe won the Ryder Cup at Oak Hill in America. Fate thrust the responsibility for the all-deciding point on the shoulders of Nick Faldo, and it looked a millstone too heavy to carry when he trailed two down on the closing holes. Eventually he needed to get down in two from 90 yards on the final hole to assure Europe of an historic success. The pressure was about as great as it can be in golf. Happily, Nick had the temperament to go with a magnificent ability. He outwardly showed the calmest of composures – though he did admit later that he inwardly felt everything was shaking – to wedge to four feet and hole the putt for the win and vital point.

Such clear thinking and calm attitude applies to many aspects of golf. In match-play it is never wise to reveal any weakness or feeling of concern to an opponent. Let him do the worrying. The mental demands of stroke-play are more exacting. This is a straight contest between the golfer and the course, and a different strategy is required to cope with the 'card and pencil' game. The great majority of club golfers find stroke-play golf more difficult than match-play simply because one is about playing the course which gives nothing away and the other involves an opponent whose own human frailties can often be encouraging.

Stroke-play or medal golf as played by the top professional is akin to chess: each shot, or move, is carefully planned. While the mind of the average amateur on the tee is so often filled with thoughts of simply hitting the fairway, the expert will be aiming at whichever side of the fairway gives him the best line into the green with his second shot. It is called 'course management', and there has been no better exponent than Jack Nicklaus whose strategic thinking made a tremendous contribution to his record of 18 major champion wins.

Watching Nicklaus think his way round a golf course is a priceless lesson. In his prime he was one of the most powerful players in the game. But he accumulated more than 100 victories as an amateur and professional by carefully harnessing that power, using it to the full only when it safely fitted into his 'game plan' or strategy. Frequently, as do today's leading tournament players, he used an iron or a 3 wood from the tee to be sure of avoiding trouble his driver might reach. Much of the enjoyment of golf is lost if the tee shot is frequently followed by a search for the ball in the rough. The first principle of golf is 'keep the ball in play' and if a great champion like Nicklaus was prepared to surrender distance for safety then there is no excuse for the average golfer who stubbornly insists on using a driver. In certain conditions, Gary Player, another collector of major championships, was never averse to using a 4-wood off the tee. These are not negative tactics, but rather positive thinking. As they both insist, brains count for more than brawn in golf.

The playing of consistently good golf requires a sound, repeating swing and a strategy based on wise thinking. The two are as inseparable as identical twins. A great swing that results in a 250-yard drive finishing in a fairway bunker is a terrible waste and the punishment for poor strategy. The psychology involved in achieving successful golf is the same at every level, be it the 18-handicap golfer aiming for an acceptable score of 90 or the world-class professional in contention for the Open Championship.

Among the greatest golfers ever, and one of the most thinking and intelligent, Australia's Peter Thomson, winner of five Open Championships, was in no doubt about the brains *vs* brawn issue. He insisted that strength was not a particular advantage. It was more important to strategically plan the playing of each hole in advance. Golf, he believed, was 50 per cent or more a mental game, and if it was accepted that the mind ultimately controls physical achievement then it was close to being entirely a mental challenge.

While winning the Ryder Cup at Oak Hill, every member of Europe's team carried the same thought on to each tee: *think before you drive.* Do the same and you could well cut six shots off your score.

Examples of course strategy at work

St Andrews, Old Course, 17th hole – 460 yards, par 4

Obviously, the standard of play expected from a professional and the average golfer varies according to their respective abilities. But their on-course strategy needs to be very similar because the overall objective for them both is to concentrate on playing each shot into a position that makes the next one as simple and easy as possible. That, in a few words, is what golf strategy is all about – hitting the ball into a position that doesn't create a problem for the following shot. There are holes on every course where it is relatively safe to attack, and there are those which the wise golfer will recognise as calling for caution because aggressiveness invites possible disaster. Take, for instance, the famous, or infamous for many who have suffered here, 17th hole on the Old Course at St Andrews, the Home of Golf.

We think it is fair to generalise and say that most golfers get into trouble at this hole because they see it is a par 4 on the card and automatically feel they must try to score a four. The sensible strategy for the average golfer would be to respect the danger and concentrate on avoiding a disaster by playing for a five while always hoping for the chance of a one-putt four.

Out of bounds on the right begins dictating this strategy. The drive needs to be down the left of the fairway, don't be tempted into the gamble of cutting corners with ambitious thoughts of getting up in

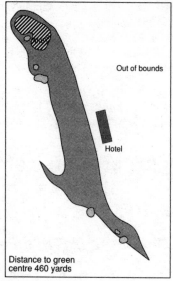

Out of bounds

Hotel

Distance to green
centre 460 yards

Respect the danger

Fig. 91 St Andrews, Old Course, 17th hole.

two. Then play the second shot short and slightly right to leave a comfortable chip up the length of the green. It's a lot safer than trying to pitch over the steep-faced greenside bunker to a narrow, angled green with the road behind waiting for the kind of overbold shot that cost Tom Watson the 1984 Open Championship.

Augusta National, Georgia, USA, 11th hole – 380 yards, par 4

This hole is the first of the three forming the renowned and difficult 'Amen Corner' at Augusta, home of the Masters tournament founded by Bobby Jones. It has been the scene of numerous tragedies and some great moments, especially for Nick Faldo, winner of two Masters titles at the 11th with play-off victories.

Ben Hogan, who at the peak of his legendary career played the most incredible golf, was never fearful of any course or challenge. But he was particularly respectful of Augusta's 11th hole, saying it was no place to gamble with attacking play.

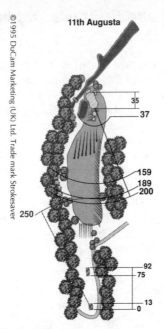

Fig. 92 Augusta National, 11th hole.

The drive is lenient enough, as most are at Augusta, but the second shot demands very careful strategy. The exceptionally fast green slopes from right to left and towards a lake. When the pin is placed well left as it usually is to add to the difficulty factor, the average golfer is then well advised to forget it, take the water out of play, and hit an approach to the right side of the green. Admittedly this encourages the risk of three putts for a bogey five, but that is a whole lot better than picking out of the water and being four with the next shot. Even missing the green on the right still allows for positive thinking. Larry Mize holed his chip to beat Greg Norman in a play-off for the 1987 Masters.

One of the most difficult things in golf, and it takes practice to master, is to play away from the pin. Instinct tells you to aim at the flag, but at times strategy demands defensive play. On the 11th at Augusta this begins with a safe drive down the left of the fairway, and this opens the way to a positional second shot to the right or 'fat' part of the green, well away from the water.

Royal Lytham and St Annes, 1st hole – 200 yards, par 3

Par 3 opening holes are rare in golf, and this is the only one on the Royal and Ancient's rota of Open Championship courses. It makes for a tough start because accuracy is vital before there has been a chance to 'warm up' and get the feel of the challenge. The last thing anyone wants is to begin a round buried in a bunker for an immediate taste of pressure. So the strategy here, once again, is to be defensive, aim for the fat of the green, settle for two putts and a par, and leave ideas of attacking golf for later. Opening holes, short or otherwise, are always a problem for the average golfer when he goes straight to the tee without a practice session. This courts trouble. A few chips, half-a-dozen putts and a couple of bunker shots, just five minutes of preparation, if that is all time allows, can make a big difference towards enjoying three hours of golf on the course.

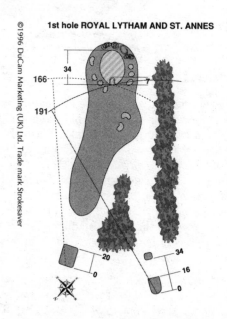

Fig. 93 Royal Lytham and St Annes, 1st hole.

The Belfry, Brabazon Course, 18th hole – 450 yards, par 4

This is one of the very best finishing holes and it has created a lot of high drama and history. Who can forget that scene of Sam Torrance with his arms raised high after making the putt that sealed Europe's 1985 Ryder Cup win. The design of the hole which calls for water to be crossed twice severely tests both ability and nerve, and without the right strategy there can be a very costly disaster. Ideally, the hole, being shaped right to left, calls for a controlled draw off the tee. That won't worry most professionals, but it is not a natural shot for most amateurs. So they should play their own game, take the water out of play as much as possible by playing the safest line across and hitting a straight drive. It might seem 'macho' to then have a go at powering the second shot over the water again, but percentage play is a vital part of good strategy. It is just as necessary for the handicap amateur to know his yardages – how far he can safely expect to hit each club – as it is the tournament professional. If the distance to be carried creates a serious risk then there is no shame in playing up short of the water to a position that makes it simple to reach the green in three. Then two

18 hole Belfry Brabazon

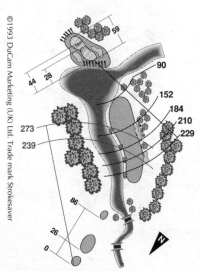

©1993 DuCam Marketing (UK) Ltd. Trade mark Strokesaver

Fig. 94 The Belfry, Brabazon Course, 18th hole.

putts mean a respectable five to complete the round, not a seven with a ball in the water as evidence of poor thinking. The big sin at a hole like this is to be too ambitious. Make up your mind on the tee to play within your limitations and remember that golf is all about concentrating on hitting your next shot to a position that makes the one after as easy as possible.

Sunningdale, Old Course, 12th hole – 425 yards, par 4

Heathland courses, like the Old at Sunningdale, will always pose special difficulties for the amateur. Miss a fairway and the ball will so often finish in heather that invites the gamble of making good distance with an aggressive recovery shot, but then turns the clubface over to inflict serious punishment for being unrealistically ambitious. When a ball nestles down in heather it is usually prudent to settle for the shortest route back to the fairway, get the ball in play again, and hope to make amends with a single putt.

12th hole SUNNINGDALE OLD COURSE

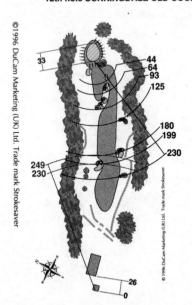

Fig. 95 Sunningdale, Old Course, 12th hole.

The 12th hole on the Old Course at Sunningdale is best respected this way and its No 1 ranking on the stroke index is well justified. It calls for two long, straight shots to a green surrounded by trouble. So the rule on the tee is look for a precise target, take perfect aim, make sure your feet and shoulders are parallel to the target, and have confidence in your swing. Once again, the strategy that dictates the second shot depends on yardage.

If the drive has left an approach that makes reaching the green in two a risky gamble, then settle for hitting short and concentrate on getting to a position that makes for a simple pitch to the flag.

Muirfield, 6th hole – 435 yards, par 4

Muirfield is a truly great links, and a favourite with many of the world's best golfers, including Jack Nicklaus who was so impressed that when he built his own course in Ohio he called it Muirfield Village. The home of the Honourable Company of Edinburgh Golfers, Muirfield, founded 10 years before the Royal and Ancient in 1744, is

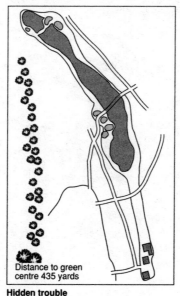

Distance to green
centre 435 yards

Hidden trouble

Fig. 96 Muirfield, 6th hole.

an established venue for the Open Championship, and its complete examination always ensures a worthy winner, as Nick Faldo, Lee Trevino, Tom Watson, Gary Player, Henry Cotton and Jack Nicklaus have proved.

The 6th hole is especially severe. A dog-leg left, there are unseen bunkers waiting for the drive. Hidden trouble is a constant problem with seaside golf which encourages 'directional' play as opposed to taking aim on a precise target. A major reason for this, of course, is that the broad expanse of a links can offer few detailed targets, like trees, on which to aim. So you have to be very careful with your lining up. It is important on a hole like Muirfield's 6th to find a spot on which to line up. You know the bunkers are there on the left but they cannot be seen, and you have to make sure of aiming away from them for the positional play needed to make the next shot easy. And remember that it's not obligatory to use the driver on a tee. If a 3 wood takes the bunker right out of play, then use it. Giving up a little distance for accuracy is no bad thing.

Wentworth, West Course, 9th hole – 430 yards, par 4

9th hole WENTWORTH WEST

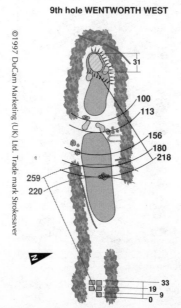

Fig. 97 Wentworth West Course, 9th hole.

This is an extremely demanding test, but there is the consolation that by the time you come to tackle its challenge you should be warmed up and ready. The shape of the hole, with the tee on the left, encourages a draw, but the amateur needs to take care to play his normal shot and not be dictated into attempting a right-to-left drive. Anything up to a 3 iron can be needed for the long second shot, and with so much trouble to be found around the green, this is where clear thinking and good strategy become all important. There is a bunker on the left, serious trouble pin-high right and through the green, so the average golfer should be thinking of clubbing down to play short, and be in position to safely chip onto the green for three. If he chips well he will have the chance to one-putt for a par four, and at worst walk off with a five, no disaster at this hole which has given some of the world's best golfers costly problems in the world match-play and PGA Championships. The message here is don't gamble by being unrealistically aggressive: to err on the negative side can be rewarding.

Royal Troon, 7th hole – 380 yards, par 4

7th hole ROYAL TROON

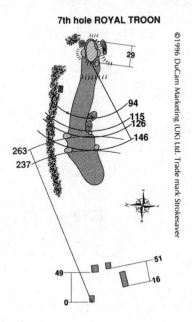

© 1996 DuCam Marketing (UK) Ltd. Trade mark Strokesaver

Fig. 98 Royal Troon, 7th hole.

One look is enough to spell out the strategy needed at this hole which is sandwiched between the longest (the 6th, 577 yards) and the shortest (8th, 126 yards) on any of the Open Championship courses. Named Tel-El-Kebir to commemorate a battle fought in Egypt in 1882, four years after the founding of the club, the 7th is most respected for its test of driving. It is imperative to take the fairway bunkers out of play. Find sand off the tee and the best you can hope for is to recover to a position where your ball would have been off a good drive. And that, on occasions, can mean hitting out sideways or even backwards to cope with the depth and steep faces of some of these seaside bunkers.

If the yardage to a fairway bunker tells you it is in range for your driver should you hit it well, then club down to a 3-wood or a long iron. It is always better to be safe than sorry in golf.

Royal St George's, 14th hole – 495 yards, par 5

J H Taylor (1894) was the first of the many great winners of the Open Championship on this outstanding course, and others since have included Harry Vardon, Henry Cotton, Bobby Locke and Sandy Lyle.

14th hole ROYAL ST. GEORGES

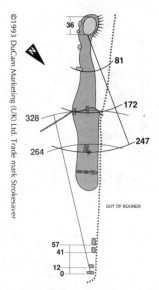

Fig. 99 Royal St Georges, 14th hole.

All paid special respect to the 14th as a hole quite capable of wrecking a potentially good score. With out of bounds on the right, where the Princes Club neighbours the fairway, it is one of Royal St George's few relatively straight holes. A helpful wind will give the professional thoughts of reaching the green in two but the average golfer has to be more concerned with keeping out of the Suez Canal, the broad stream which crosses the fairway some 340 yards from the tee. On the tee he has to think 'I'll be happy with a five' and decide his strategy on the basis of not being too ambitious. He has to be satisfied with avoiding sand land out-of-bounds with his drive, and then making absolutely sure of getting over the water in two.

If he hits a poor drive into the rough then he must accept his own limitations, and avoid the temptation to try and make up for it with a super second – the odds are he will be picking the ball out of the water and playing four with his next shot. It might well be prudent to lay up, play a cautious second short of the Suez Canal, and still leave a fair chance of getting down in three more from around 170 yards.

Woburn, Duke's Course, 13th hole – 420 yards, par 4

Pines punish a drive too far left, so the strategy here is keep right off the tee and then make sure of taking enough club to carry a deep gully and a bunker protecting the green. This is a hole on which you have to be aggressive so correct club selection is important. Course yardage books are very helpful in this respect, but you do need to know to reasonably accurate limits just how far you hit each club in the bag, especially the mid irons. But how many amateurs do? Sadly, not too many. Yet it is easy enough to determine with time well spent on the practice ground, and the reward can be any number of valuable shots saved. The top tournament professional will know, for example, that he hits his 5-iron 175 yards on average.

It is imperative for the amateur, no matter what his general standard of play, to have the confidence that comes from being able to select the right club, and for this he needs to know his own yardage limits. When he has this ability he can use yardage books and begin to plan his course strategy like a professional. Avoiding disasters – taking two and three over par – is the key to playing to your handicap, and good thinking for wise strategy is the way to go.

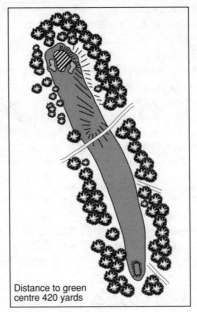

Distance to green
centre 420 yards

Be aggressive

Fig. 100 Woburn, Duke's Course, 13th hole.

17

EVERY GOLFER'S 'GURU' – THE CLUB PROFESSIONAL

Tournament golf, as the shop window for the game, makes household names of the likes of Jack Nicklaus, Nick Faldo, Bernhard Langer, and their fellow champions. But they are the first to recognise and acclaim that the popularity of golf owes so much to the largely unsung work of the club professional. He and she – there are now more than 100 lady club professionals – play many vital roles to encourage the ever-increasing number of amateurs on whose enthusiasm the sport thrives.

The club professional, with his teaching skills, experienced advice on everything from how to cure a slice to advanced agronomy, and a well-stocked shop offering expert service, makes a massively important contribution to golf. He may not create the headlines of a championship winner, but his grass-roots involvement is no less important. Beginners and advanced golfers alike can benefit greatly by making good use of all that the friendly club professional has to offer. He, more than anyone, has the ability to help the golfer maximise his enjoyment of the game for life.

The Professional Golfers' Association was founded in 1901 to unite professional golfers into a uniform body serving the needs of club golfers throughout the British Isles. Although the role of club professional has changed radically, that main fundamental has stayed constant for almost 100 years with amateurs of all playing levels benefiting from his skills and knowledge.

In the early days the professional mostly emerged from the caddie ranks and as they developed an aptitude for the game, they would pit their ability against other professionals in challenge matches and the very occasional tournament. There was no regular tournament schedule as there is today, and so a professional would become attached to a club which would be his primary source of income. This practice continued until after the Second World War when an embryonic tournament circuit began, but even then events were arranged to finish on a Friday so that the competing professional could hurry back to his club and look after the needs of the members over the weekend.

Now the career path of a professional is clearly defined. Those who have the ambition to make a living by playing tournaments can try to gain PGA European Tour membership at an annual qualifying school, and hundreds compete every year for a very limited number of places. Those who see their vocation as club professionals serve a three-year apprenticeship as an assistant working under a fully qualified professional at a club. It is a rigorous introduction to a demanding career. This grounding will cover all aspects of club professional life, from serving members in the professional's shop, to teaching, playing with members and, essentially, offering them sound advice on the most suitable equipment for their game.

The professional at any club is a vital part of the club's everyday life. He is there for long hours, ready to assist any member on any aspect of his game and provide a shop stocked with the latest in equipment and clothing. And he becomes a friend to all, someone to be trusted, respected and whose knowledge of the game is invaluable, especially when the average golfer comes to buy costly equipment with the hope of improving his standard of play and therefore his enjoyment. Buying an unsuitable set of clubs is the worst disaster in golf, but is easily avoided with the advice of the experienced club professional.

In most clubs there is usually a thriving junior section and it is here that many dedicated professionals build for the future by providing group lessons through the Golf Foundation, the national body for the development of junior golf. The benefits of the project cannot be over-emphasised as it means that each boy and girl involved receives a solid grounding in proper techniques and, through the Golf Foundation Merit Scheme, is rewarded as they progress. Instruction is also given on the rules and etiquette so that juniors can go on to be valuable full members of a club. Many who have received Golf Foundation coaching have achieved success as amateurs and professionals.

It can be seen and appreciated, therefore, that the role of the club professional is high among the most important in the game. As the appeal of golf has grown with more and more newcomers to the game, so the club professional has become a respected mentor, guide, adviser and friend to them all. Make good use of all that he has to offer to be sure of enjoying golf to the full.

GLOSSARY OF GOLFING TERMS

ace Hole in one, a feat with odds of 40,000–1 against for the average golfer.

address Positioning of the body and club in readiness to play a shot.

air shot To swing and miss the ball.

albatross Score of three under par on one hole, i.e. to hole in one at a par four or in two shots at a par five.

all square State of tied match.

approach shot Any stroke played with the intention of putting the ball on the green.

apron Mown area immediately surrounding green.

arc Path taken by clubhead throughout swing.

assistant Trainee professional golfer.

away The ball farthest from the hole is said to be away.

back holes Second half of the course, i.e. last nine holes.

back marker Player with the lowest handicap in the group.

backspin Clockwise spinning action imparted on the ball by the lofted and grooved face of a club to help control its flight and roll.

backswing Movement of body and club from address position to top of the swing.

back tee Slang for championship tee.

baffy Obsolete wooden club equivalent to No 4 wood.

ball American-sized ball of 42.67 mm (1.68 inches) is in the process of completely replacing the British ball of 41.15 mm (1.62 inches) diameter. Both weigh 45.92 grams (1.62 ounces).

ball marker Plastic disc or small coin used to mark precise position of ball on green before lifting to clean.

better-ball match A match in which two partners form a team and only the better score of either player counts at each hole.

birdie Score of one below par.

bisque Handicap stroke that can be claimed at any hole during a match.

blade Striking area of iron club.

blading Term for a topped shot that causes the ball to fly low or run along the ground.

blaster Slang name for a wedge.

blind shot Hitting to a target hidden by rising ground, trees or other course feature.

bogey First introduced as the score a first-class amateur should make at each hole. Now universally recognised as denoting a score of one shot more than par, e.g. taking five strokes at a par four hole. Six shots would be a *double bogey*.

borrow Aiming to one side of the hole by varying amounts to allow for the contours of a green when putting – 'Borrow two feet to the left.' Also known as break.

brassey/brassie Name for a No 2 wood club which has fallen out of fashion.

break See *borrow*

bulger Driver with convex face.

bunker Depression in the ground filled with sand – an intended and maintained hazard.

buggy Colloquial term for motorised golf cart.

bye Secondary and informal match played over holes remaining to the 18th when the main game is completed.

caddie Person engaged to carry player's clubs and offer advice when asked.

caddie cart Two-wheeled trolley for carrying clubs.

callaway Handicapping system in which a player's score is determined by his worst holes.

card Official score card of the course.

carry Distance from where the ball is hit to where it lands.

casual water Temporary accumulation of water, snow or ice on the course, not forming any part of a declared water hazard, and from which a player is allowed to lift the ball clear without penalty.

centre shaft Club with shaft fitted to centre of head.

chip Short, low-running shot.

choke Slang term for losing one's nerve.

choke down Hold the club with hands lower than usual on the grip for short, delicate shots, or to reduce the distance potential of a full shot.

cleat Metal stud for golf shoes.

cleek Old iron club equivalent to No 2 iron.

closed clubface Club aimed left of target at address.

closed stance Player's body is aimed right of target with right foot drawn back behind left at address position.

clubface Lofted and grooved area of clubhead with which ball is hit.

concede Term of surrender – putt, hole or match.

course Ground within clearly defined boundaries on which game is played.

cup Colloquial term for the hole.

cut See *slice*

cut-up-shot Sidespin deliberately imparted to give the ball a curving flight from left to right.

dead See *gimme*

dimples Indentations – averaging 330 – on the cover of a golf ball designed to maximise its aerodynamic qualities.

divot Turf cut from under ball in the playing of an iron shot.

dog-leg Hole designed with angled fairway.

dog licence Slang for 7/6 result in match play contest – derived from seven shillings and sixpence once being the cost of a dog licence.

dormey/dormie Situation in match play when a player cannot be beaten because he leads the same number of holes as there are still left to play.

driving range Area specifically designed and maintained for practice.

downswing Movement of body and club from top of swing to point of impact.

draw shot Controlled right-to-left curving flight.

driver Club designed with minimum loft to give tee shots maximum distance.

drive the green Hit a tee shot that reaches the green.

duck hook Shot that curves sharply to the left of target line.

eagle Score of two shots under par at one hole, e.g. three at a par five.

eclectic Best score at each hole on one course over a number of rounds.

equity Method of resolving disputes not covered by rules.

etiquette The code of good manners, sportsmanship and respect for other players on the course that upholds the tradition of golf being a game for gentlemen.

explosion shot Recovery stroke from bunker which calls for hitting the sand rather than ball.

fade Controlled left-to-right flight.

fairway Mown grass between tee and green.

fat shot Hitting ground behind ball instead of making clean contact.

featherie/feathery Ball, which replaced the original wooden ball, with a leather cover stuffed tight with feathers, used until about 1848, and now a valuable collectors' item.

flagstick Pole of six feet or more in height, bearing flag, which signifies position of hole on each green.

flange Ridge along base of iron club or putter.

flat swing Act of swinging the club on a plane nearer to being horizontal than vertical.

flier Shot lacking backspin to control flight and roll – usually the result of playing from rough where the thick grass forms a cushion between clubface and ball at impact.

fluff A bad mishit

follow-though Continuation of the swing after impact.

fore Warning cry of 'Fore' is shouted by golfer to alert others in danger of being hit by ball.

forward press Slight movement of the hands – not the clubhead – at the address position to guard against tension.

fourball Match involving four players, each playing his own game, though two may form a partnership for a *better* score.

foursomes Two players in partnership hit alternate shots with one ball.

fried egg lie Ball half buried in bunker.

gimme Putt so short that it is considered unmissable and worthy of being conceded in match play golf. In stroke play or medal golf all putts have to be holed. Gimmie putts are also known as *dead*.

grain See *nap*

grand slam First used to describe the 1930 unique achievement of Bobby Jones winning the Open and Amateur Championships of Britain and the United States. Now updated to mean the Open Championships conducted by the Royal and Ancient Golf Club of St Andrews; and the US Masters, Open and PGA Championships.

green Those areas of a course specifically prepared for putting. Also the original name for a course, that form surviving in the terms green fee, green committee.

greensome Informal format which calls for both players forming a partnership to drive and then select the better-placed ball to continue playing the hole by hitting alternate shots in foursomes fashion.

grip Method of holding a club or the 'handle' of a club

ground under repair Areas of course officially marked as unfit for play and from which a golfer is entitled to move his ball without penalty.

guttie/gutty Solid golf ball made of gutta-percha, a rubbery substance, which replaced the *feathery* and was in use until the early 1900s.

half Opponents have 'halved' when they complete a hole in the same number of shots or finish a match tied.

handicap Official allowance of shots based on a golfer's average performance against the scratch score of a course, a system that allows players of all standards to compete with each other on equal terms.

hanging lie Shot that has to be played off sloping ground.

haskell Forerunner of the modern golf ball, rubber-cored, introduced early 1900s to replace the *gutty*. Named after the American Coburn Haskell who invented a machine to wind rubber thread under tension around a central core.

hazards Bunkers or any intended areas of water on the course.

head The striking part of a club.

heel Angle formed by neck and face of a club.

hickory Type of wood used to make golf club shafts before steel shafts were legalised in 1929 (1924 in USA).

hitting early Starting to uncock the wrists too soon in the downswing.

hitting late Delaying the uncocking of the wrists in an attempt to increase clubhead acceleration and therefore hit the ball a greater distance.

hole Rules decree that it must be 4¼ inches (108 mm) in diameter and at least 4 inches (100 mm) deep.

hole in one Hitting tee shot into the hole.

home of golf Traditional reference to St Andrews, in Scotland.

honour The right to play first from the tee – a matter of agreement at the start of a match but thereafter the honour automatically goes to the player who did best at the previous hole. In the event of a hole being halved then the player who held the honour retains it.

hooding Rotating the face of the club towards the target, thereby reducing the normal lift.

hook Shot with sidespin that causes pronounced right-to-left flight.

hosel Neck or socket in which the shaft joins the clubhead.

impact Precise point at which clubface strikes the ball.

in play A ball is 'in play' from the moment it has been struck on the tee until it comes to rest in the hole.

irons Clubs with metal heads and faces with lofts varied in sequence to determine trajectory and distance of shots.

jigger Utility club once popular for playing chip shots.

jungle Slang for trees, bushes, heavy rough or any punishing form of natural growth bordering fairways.

lag Long putt played cautiously with intention of leaving the ball close to the hole (as opposed to a bold, attacking stroke in an attempt to hole out at the risk of running past the hole if unsuccessful).

lie Situation of the ball at rest – a *good lie* if 'sitting up' well on the fairway; *a bare (barefaced) lie* if on a pathway or some other worn surface; a *bad lie* if in thick grass, a divot or similar trouble. Also describes angle between shaft and clubhead.

line Direction in which a shot needs to be hit.

links Golf course built on sandy, seaside terrain.
lip Edge or rim of the hole – a ball which hits the hole but fails to fall in is said to have 'lipped' out.
local knowledge Advantage enjoyed by a player competing on a course he knows well.
local rules Additional rules to meet specific circumstances at every course.
loft Angle of the clubface.
loose impediments Natural objects – stones, leaves, litter etc – that player is allowed to remove when they hamper his ability to hit the ball.
lost ball A ball is officially lost if it cannot be found within five minutes.

marker Person designated to keep score.
mashie Old iron club equivalent to No 5 iron.
match play Contest decided on the winning of individual holes.
medal play Contest decided on the total number of strokes taken to complete the course, more correctly called stroke-play.
mixed foursome Partnership of one man and one woman hitting alternate shots with one ball.
municipal course Operated by the local authority for the general public – as opposed to private club – and an ideal starting point for newcomers to golf.
mulligan Allowing a player starting a game to hit a second drive if he is dissatisfied with his first. Not condoned by the rules.
muscle memory Automatic observance of correct swing movements developed by disciplined and repetitive practice.

nap Tendency of grass to grow at an angle and influence the roll of the ball on greens. Also known as grain.
nassau Dividing one round of golf into three separate matches for betting purposes – first nine holes, back nine, and over-all 18.
never up, never in Term of condemnation for putting short of hole.
niblick Old club equivalent to No 8 iron.
nineteenth First extra hole to decide tied match or, more generally, colloquial expression for clubhouse bar.

obstructions Man-made objects from which the golfer is entitled to relief.
open stance Left foot drawn back so that player's body is turned slightly towards target at position of address.
out of bounds All areas outside the defined limits of the course.
outside agency Any agency, person or animal, not competitively involved in a match, e.g. referee, observer, steward – but liable to accidentally obstruct or move ball.

par Indicates score a scratch handicap golfer is expected to make at a hole –
i.e. holes up to 250 yards (228 metres) in length are rated as par 3s; between
251 yards and 475 yards (434 metres) inclusive as par 4s; and anything
longer as par 5.

penalty stroke Added to score for taking relief under the rules or infringing
rules.

persimmon Hardwood specially favoured for the making of clubheads.

PGA Professional Golfers' Association.

pick and drop Act of picking ball up and dropping it in another spot as
allowed by the rules in specified circumstances, e.g. taking relief from casual
water and unplayable lie.

pin Slang term for flagstick.

pin high Ball that comes to rest level with the flagstick, either on or off the
green.

pitch Short, high shot. Hence, pitching wedge.

pitch mark Indentation made by ball hitting ground. Etiquette demands
that a player always repairs his pitch mark on a green.

pivot Turning of body in the backswing.

plane Angle at which the club is swung, in relation to the ground.

play off Extra hole or holes played to settle a tie.

plugged Ball embedded in its own pitch mark.

preferred lie Right to improve lie of the ball under temporary local rule
intended to offset abnormal ground conditions.

press The fault of trying to hit the ball too hard; also a form of gambling –
generally accepted as claiming the right to strike an extra wager on going two
down in a match.

provisional ball Playing second ball to save time when suspecting that first
might be lost or out of bounds.

pull Ball flying straight left of target.

punch Shot played with short backswing and hands ahead of ball at impact
to keep ball on low trajectory.

push Ball flying straight right of target.

putt Shot made with a putter on a green.

putter straight-faced club designed for use on greens.

quail high shot Extremely low-flying shot.

quit on shot Failure to continue the swing after impact.

rabbit Novice player.

rap Deliberate putting style which calls for short, decisive stroke and stop-
ping blade of putter at impact.

recovery shot Hitting ball to safety from position of trouble.

regulation Number of shots appropriate to hole by a good golfer.

relief To take relief is to pick up the ball and drop it in another spot as allowed by the rules in specified (unplayable) circumstances.

rough Long grass cultivated to punish shots which miss the fairways or greens.

round robin Match play competition in which every competitor plays all the others, the one achieving the most victories being the overall winner.

Royal and Ancient The Royal and Ancient Golf Club of St Andrews, the governing body of the game throughout most of the world.

rub of the green Golfing luck, good or bad, created by an eccentric bounce or outside agency influencing the outcome of a shot and for which there is no provision under the rules.

run Distance a ball travels after it pitches.

run up shot Low shot into the green with the intention of having the ball roll to the hole as opposed to a lofted pitch.

Ryder Cup Biennial team match between players from the PGA European Tour and the United States PGA Tour.

sand iron Club with broad, rounded sole and extremely lofted face, specifically designed for bunker shots.

scratch A scratch golfer is one with zero handicap.

senior Professional golfers are officially recognised as seniors (or *veterans*) for tournament purposes on reaching the age of 50, and amateurs at 55.

single Match between two players.

shank Shot when contact is made with the neck of the club, causing the ball to fly off at an eccentric angle. Also known as a socket.

sky To hit an exceptionally high but short shot.

slice Shot that sends ball flying in a pronounced left-to-right curve. Also known as a cut.

socket See *shank*

sole Base of club head.

split hand Putting method with hands kept apart to grip club.

spoon Old wooden club equivalent to No 3 wood.

square stance Both feet are parallel to the target line at the address position.

Stableford Competition format based on points – one point at every hole the player scores a net one-over-par bogey; two points for a par; three points for a birdie, four points for an eagle; five points for an albatross. Invented by Dr Frank Stableford, member of the Royal Liverpool and Wallasey Clubs, in 1931.

stance The act of a player placing his feet in position in readiness to hit the ball.

standard scratch score Every course has an SSS rating based on length and difficulty, and this becomes the score a scratch golfer is expected to make in fair weather.

stroke The act of intentionally hitting the ball.

stroke hole Where a player receives or gives a stroke to his opponents under the handicapping system.

stroke index Chart detailing stroke holes in order of priority.

stroke play Also known as medal play, or card-and-pencil golf. An examination of how many shots a player needs to complete the course.

sudden death Play-off to decide a tie.

swingweight Ratio of weight, length and balance intended to ensure that all clubs in a set are perfectly matched.

takeaway Start of the backswing.

tee Prepared area from which golfer begins to play every hole.

tee marker Usually a box, cone or plaque indicating exactly where on the tee the drive must be hit.

tee peg Wooden or plastic aid on which ball can be perched for tee shots only.

tempo Rhythm vital to a good swing.

texas wedge American expression applied to a putter when used off the green for an approach shot.

threeball Three players forming a match.

through the green All of the course except teeing grounds, greens and hazards.

tiger Golfer of high ability.

topping Hitting top half of the ball so that it scuttles along the ground.

topspin Also called overspin, opposite of backspin, intended to make the ball run a maximum distance.

tradesman's entrance Back or side edge of the hole.

trolley Caddie cart for carrying clubs.

trap Slang: bunkers are known as traps on American courses.

turn Position reached after nine holes.

upright swing Act of swinging club more towards the vertical than horizontal.

valley of sin Famous hollow in front of the 18th green on the Old Course at St Andrews, in Scotland.

Vardon grip Method of holding club popularised by Harry Vardon, winner of the Open Championship six times between 1896 and 1914.

velocity Manufacture of golf balls is governed by a velocity rule with a limit of 250 feet (76.2 metres) per second.

veteran See *senior*

waggle Movement of hands and clubhead at address position to release tension while establishing sense of 'feel' and rhythm.

Walker Cup Biennial amateur team match between Britain and Ireland, and the United States.

water hazard Any sea, lake, pond, river, ditch, surface drainage ditch or other open water course whether or not containing water, and anything of a similar nature.

wedge Broad-sole, lofted club used for short, high pitches and a variety of trouble shots.

whipping Twine or filament binding to secure heads of wooden clubs.

winter rules Temporary concessions – such as allowing the ball to be picked up and cleaned on the fairways – to make play possible and protect the course against undue wear in abnormal conditions.

wry neck Club with curved neck.

yardage chart Personal measurements, listing landmarks on each hole of a course to help a player judge the distance of any shot.

yips A nervous affliction which makes controlling the hands difficult, especially when putting. Also known as the twitch.

INDEX